CONTENTS

LIST OF TABLES

FIGURE

FOREWORD

The election of Ronald Reagan to the U.S. Presidency in 1980 was a statement by the American people that their government has become too large, too expensive, and too intrusive. It is now time to translate that mandate into pragmatic, sensible actions to bring about responsible change in the boundaries that separate the sovereignty of the individual and private institutions from the sovereignty of government.

This book provides the reader with a conceptual framework for identifying the goods and services society wants and needs; what is more important, it provides guidelines for increasing nongovernmental means to meet them. In a healthy balance between theory and examples, the author details how many services currently provided by the public sector can be privatized or re-privatized.

Given the broad goals of Reagan Federalism, the issues addressed in this book are likely to continue to be a focus of public debate in the future. The book ends with a practical blueprint for reducing the size and scope of government that all thoughtful citizens — elected officials and taxpayers alike — can act upon, or at least argue about in an enlightened debate.

MARTIN ANDERSON
Assistant to the President
for Policy Development
The White House

CHAPTER 1

INTRODUCTION

Government is in trouble in the United States. Trust in government declined dramatically from almost 80 percent in the late 1950s to about 33 percent in the mid-'70s. About three out of five people believe that government has too much power concentrated in too few hands. Even before the revelations of Abscam, fewer than one person in five felt that congressional leaders could be believed.[1] In short, government has lost the confidence and faith of the people. Cynics and skeptics see government merely as a bumbling bureaucracy interfering with and annoying hard-working, ordinary people while engaging in ever more inconsistent and misguided behavior that is ludicrous when it doesn't hit too close to home. Or else they look on government as an evil to which they have perforce become accustomed, an exploiting force out of control, a horde of self-aggrandizing opportunists — elected officials, civil servants, and unionized public employees alike.

This attitude is not the familiar grumbling about death and taxes. It is something deeper, and it is much more dangerous. Government is a social contract between citizens. The functionaries of democratic government, from dogcatchers to Presidents, derive their rightful powers from the willing consent of the governed. That consent has been withdrawn — not formally but, more important, in people's minds and hearts — to a discernible and significant degree. Evading the spirit of government-inspired laws has become a legitimate game played by all. At the big-money table, the game has high entry stakes, but no matter—the stakes are waived by the government: Anyone can take deductions to pay lawyers and lobbyists to connive and cajole on his or her behalf. At the cheaper tables, anomie is more evident, in the "off-the-books economy" and in the behavior of tax-evading businessmen, feral teenagers, unemployment insurance chiselers, pooper-scooperless dog walkers, welfare cheats, college graduates who default on their tuition loans, and aged widows who hide their assets to qualify for public benefits.

The election of Ronald Reagan as President and the strong support for his initial efforts to cut back the size and scope of the federal government are reflections of a broad-based reaction against the current role of government. A constructive interpretation of this reaction[2] is that (1) the huge job of government—begun a century ago—of building the nation and integrating its parts, of allocating the costs and benefits of change and progress, of correcting the major abuses of business, and of alleviating human problems and improving the lot of the populace, has largely been completed; and (2) the reforms of a generation ago are themselves sorely in need of reform, as mistakes, excesses, waste, and scandals appear, and as the inevitable institutional arteriosclerosis sets in.

The purpose of this book is to present a way of thinking about the proper role of government that, if it seeps into the public's consciousness and succeeds in influencing attitudes and actions, can contribute to a gradual change for the better.

Chapter 2 briefly summarizes some facts about the size and growth of government in the United States, and explains why government poses a threat to democracy. As more and more of the people's earnings are taken by government, as decisions about the disposition of these moneys are made by increasingly distant and unresponsive organs of government, and as government's presence pervades more and more areas of human activity, the loss of freedom becomes palpable. In drawing up the Constitution and the Bill of Rights, America's founding fathers took great pains to protect the citizens from their government. The history of civilization clearly showed that government could be a serious threat to the individual rights they cherished. Even in a democratic society, government institutions could become instruments of tyranny; those who mobilized majority support could use government's coercive sanctions to deprive those in the minority. Therefore, the framers of the Constitution designed a system that imposed the minimal level of collective coercion necessary to secure the blessings of liberty. At each turn the power of government was circumscribed by checks and balances.

Seen from another perspective, modern civilization requires individuals to cede substantial control over vital aspects of their lives to impersonal institutions. Individual autonomy has been reduced, and the responsibility for the well-being of the individuals has been assumed by collective institutions — principally government. But if the latter is not sufficiently responsive or accountable, and if it acquires a life of its own, then people feel that it is not living up to its end of an implied agreement, namely, to do those things that only it is supposed to be able to do; and they lose faith in it. "I trusted you with my well-being and you have violated that trust because you are concerned only with your own narrow, selfish interests," seems to be what people are saying about their government.[3]

Freedom and individual liberty are not the only values endangered by powerful governments. Justice is also a good we rightly prize, and equality is an important component of justice. Reasonable and humane people differ on the degree of inequality or the extent of redistribution that is acceptable and can still be considered just, but it is clear that government greatly affects the level of justice, for better and for worse, by taking from some and giving to others.

In a world of finite resources, efficiency is also an important societal goal. One should extract the maximum from each ton of raw material and from each hour of work. Efficiency is good because it produces a higher standard of living. Just as freedom and justice can be menaced by an overly powerful government, so can efficiency.

Freedom, justice, and efficiency are all essential, and each is alloyed with the other. They are multiple and conflicting goals, and we must accept a balance among them, for example, trading off some individual freedom or some economic efficiency for more justice. Government is a tool that society employs to help attain these goals and to strike the balance, even though in excess it threatens all three goals.

But government is only one tool or institution for achieving these goals. There are others, too, such as the family, close associations of like-minded individuals, religious institutions, and the marketplace. Here lies a further peril. A large and powerful government can displace and swamp these other institutions. The family may give way to Departments of Health, Education, Welfare, and Human Services. The priest, minister, and rabbi can be replaced by a community mental health agency. Voluntary groups can be supplanted by issue-oriented lobbies that seek to use the force and majesty of government to impose their values on others.

These other institutions provide safety to society by their very redundance, and help arrive at an adaptive equilibrium among the conflicting goals of freedom, justice, and efficiency. To the extent that one institution, such as government, gains great strength at the expense of the other institutions, it limits their contribution to these goals, eliminates the diversity they afford, and thereby increases society's dependence on government alone to choose and impose particular quotas of freedom, justice, and efficiency.[4]

This book takes the position that it is possible to check the growth of government and to reduce unwarranted and unwanted dependence on government agencies, thereby mitigating the hazards that an overly dominant government represents.

To understand how to accomplish this, it is necessary to start at the beginning and to examine the basic goods and services that people need. This is done in chapter 3, where it is shown that the various goods and services have intrinsic characteristics that permit them to be categorized in a particularly useful way. Chapter 4 goes on to clarify the role of collective action in supplying certain categories of goods. Then the chapter describes nine different institutional arrangements or structures used to deliver goods and services: government provision, intergovernmental agreements, franchising, contracting for service, voucher systems, grants, voluntary mutual-aid associations, self-help or self-service, and the marketplace.

Chapter 5 shows that each category of goods and services can be delivered by any one of several of the delivery arrangements, although certain arrangements cannot be used to supply certain kinds of goods. There follows an extended comparison of the different service arrangements, pointing out the advantages and disadvantages of each and shedding light on the question of which arrangement to use when there is a choice.

The recurrent and hotly debated issue of public versus private provision of service is discussed in chapter 6. After listing the putative advantages of contracting for services and of having government agencies provide services directly, the empirical evidence—such as it is—is presented for many different functions.

Chapter 7 concludes by summarizing the proposed cure, a multipronged approach that would (1) reduce government provision or subsidization of certain services; (2) make greater use of those service-delivery arrangements that require a lesser role for government; (3) employ user charges to make costs more visible; and (4) utilize competition to the fullest possible extent to overcome the harmful consequences of unnecessary government monopolies.

The book calls for reconsidering the respective roles and responsibilities of government, the individual, the family, voluntary associations, private firms, and the marketplace. It demonstrates that public services can be provided through several alternative institutional means, including some that permit greater reliance on private initiatives and require a more modest role for government than is often — thoughtlessly — deemed necessary. Broader recognition of these principles can bring about more limited and more sensible government — and hence greater freedom, justice, and efficiency — without sacrificing the advances of the last half century. This promises a restoration of legitimacy and a greater measure of public trust in democratic government.

NOTES

1. Daniel Yankelovich, "The Private and the Public Ethic: How It Is Changing" (address delivered at the annual dinner of the University Seminars, Columbia University, 20 April 1977).
2. See "Enlarging Our Capacity to Adapt" (report of the Committee on Issues of the 80s, Citizens League, Minneapolis, Minn., 1980), pp. 5-8.
3. Yankelovich, "Private and Public Ethic."
4. Victor R. Fuchs, "The Economics of Health in a Post-Industrial Society," *Public Interest*, no. 56 (Summer 1979): 3-20.

CHAPTER 2

THE GROWTH
OF
GOVERNMENT

Governments have grown in both democratic and totalitarian systems, in capitalist and in socialist countries. This chapter first examines the size and growth of government in the United States by reference to the number of government units, their expenditures, and the number of people they employ. The remainder of the chapter then explores the reasons why government has grown.

NUMBER OF GOVERNMENTS

People sometimes think of government as a single, monolithic giant, but in fact there are many governments in the United States, 79,913 of them in 1977 to be exact. Table 2.1 shows the number of different government units and how it has changed over time. The number of municipalities has been growing slowly, an indication of increasing urbanization and the accompanying incorporation of previously unincorporated areas. The number of special districts shows a more rapid growth, a reflection of the continuous creation of intergovernmental arrangements to perform various functions in metropolitan areas. In fact, this has caused an upturn in the total number of government units, after a sharper and prolonged decline that resulted from the extensive consolidation of school districts.

7

TABLE 2.1

Number of Government Units in the United States

Kind of Government	1942	1952	1962	1972	1977
Federal	1	1	1	1	1
State	48	48	50	50	50
County	3,050	3,049	3,043	3,044	3,042
Town and township	18,919	17,202	17,142	16,991	16,822
Municipal	16,220	16,778	18,000	18,517	18,862
School district	108,579	67,346	34,678	15,781	15,174
Special district	8,299	12,319	18,323	23,885	25,962
TOTAL	155,116	116,743	91,237	78,269	79,913

SOURCE: Bureau of the Census.

GOVERNMENT EXPENDITURES

Total government expenditures in 1980 amounted to $868.5 billion. Table 2.2 on page 9 shows the growth of these expenditures. In fifty years, government expenditures have grown eighty-fold, from an eighth to a third of the gross national product (GNP). Even when adjusted by subtracting expenditures for national defense and for veterans' benefits, the growth pattern remains unchanged. Per capita expenditures, adjusted in this manner and expressed in constant dollars, have increased more than fivefold during the period.

The growth has not occurred uniformly at all levels of government. Federal expenditures have grown much more rapidly than nonfederal ones, and state expenditures in turn have grown more rapidly than local ones; therefore the latter have been shrinking steadily in relative terms. This represents an increasing centralization of power at higher levels of government and, by contrast, a waning of local government.

TAX LEVELS

International comparisons can be made by examining tax revenue in relation to the gross national product in different coun-

TABLE 2.2
Government Expenditures, Including Federal, State, and Local

(1) Year	(2) Total (billions)	(3) As percent of GNP	(4) Total, excluding national defense and veteran expenditures (billions)	(5) (4) as percent of GNP	(6) (4) in constant 1972 dollars (billions)	(7) (4) as per capita expenditures in constant 1972 dollars
1930	$11.1	12.2	$9.6	10.6	$45.1	$367
1940	18.4	18.4	16.3	16.3	75.5	572
1950	61.0	21.3	41.4	14.5	105.1	691
1960	136.4	27.0	85.1	16.8	146.7	810
1970	313.4	31.6	224.6	22.9	256.7	1252
1980	869.0	33.1	704.0	26.8	381.8	1681

SOURCE: Derived from *Facts and Figures on Government Finance* (20th ed.; New York: Tax Foundation, 1979), tables 20 and 51; *Facts and Figures on Government Finance* (21st ed.; Washington, D.C.: Tax Foundation, 1981), table 23; *Survey of Current Business*, Bureau of Economic Analysis, U.S. Department of Commerce; *Economic Report of the President*, Council of Economic Advisers, February 1982; and Special Analyses, Budget of the U.S. Government, Fiscal Year 1982, Office of Management and Budget.

tries. Table 2.3 presents this comparison and shows the United States to be in the lower half of the range of industrialized nations. However, Drucker points out that in Western Europe the tax burden includes essentially all expenditures for health care and most expenditures that in the United States are paid privately for parochial schools and higher education.[1] If these private expenditures are added to the tax burden in the United States, thereby making the statistics more comparable, the revised figure would place the United States somewhere around the bottom of the list. To illustrate, Drucker calculated that for California residents (prior to the passage of Proposition 13), the combined federal, state, and local tax burden, combined with expenses for nongovernmental health care and private education, amounted to half the per capita income.

TABLE 2.3
Tax Revenue as Percent of GNP, 1978

Country	Tax Revenue
Spain	22.8%
Japan	24.1
Greece	28.1
Australia	28.8
United States	30.2
Canada	31.1
Switzerland	31.5
Italy	32.6
United Kingdom	34.5
West Germany	37.8
France	39.7
Austria	41.4
Sweden	53.5

SOURCE: *Facts and Figures on Government Finance* (21st ed.; Washington, DC: 1981), table 25.

GOVERNMENT EMPLOYMENT

Corroborating evidence concerning the size and growth of government can be found in the employment data of table 2.4.

In 1979, the number of full-time-equivalent government employees, not counting the military, was 14.0 million, or about one out of every seven nonagricultural civilian workers. (If part-time workers are included the total is 17.4 million; if military personnel are added the total is 20.2 million, or about 22 percent of the total nonagricultural work force.) In addition, the number of employees of private firms working for the federal government is estimated to be another 3.0 to 4.0 million.[2] Since 1949 the government work force has grown at a compounded annual rate of 3.4 percent, more than twice that of the population as a whole (1.4 percent) and almost twice that of private-sector employment (1.8 percent).

TABLE 2.4

Government Employment

Number of Government Employees

Year	In Millions[a]	As Percent of Population	As Percent of All Employees[b]
1929	2.92	2.39	8.2
1939	5.79	4.42	16.1
1949	5.59	3.75	12.2
1960	7.90	4.37	14.5
1970	11.35	5.54	16.6
1979	13.96	6.22	14.9

SOURCE: *Facts and Figures* (see table 2.2 for citation), 19th and 21st eds., tables 12 and 14.

[a] Full-time equivalents, excluding military.
[b] Includes only nonagricultural civilian workers.

WHY GOVERNMENT GROWS

Three major factors have contributed to the observed growth of government: (1) a demand for more government services, by recipients of the services; (2) a desire to supply more government services, by the producers of the services; (3) increased inefficiency, which results in more government spending to provide the same services. Each of these is discussed in turn.

Increased Demand for Services

Population Change. Inflation, population growth, and an increase in defense-related expenditures account for much of the absolute growth of government, but, as table 2.2 showed, the real growth was large even after allowing for these effects. Part of the explanation has to do with a change in the composition of the population to one that demands more government services. For example, if the number of retired old people increases relative to the number of working adults, and if pension payments of constant size in constant dollars are made to them out of general government funds rather than from an actuarially sound retirement fund, government expenditures will increase even if all else remains unchanged.

The same phenomenon can be observed at the local government level, when the population of a city changes so that a larger fraction of its residents are welfare recipients even though population size itself remains unchanged. Faced with this increased demand, welfare and welfare-related expenditures will rise to accommodate the increased workload. Yet this explains only part of the observed increase. A study of this issue in New York City found that during the period from 1960 to 1970 only 40 percent of the $3.9 billion increase in the human services budget was the result of inflation and a larger workload; 60 percent was due to other factors.[3]

Urbanization creates a demand for services. As urbanization increases, people get in each other's way. More police officers are needed. New kinds of government action are called for to regulate and ameliorate harmful and potentially harmful side effects of individual actions—for instance, to monitor and control air and water pollution; to reduce noise; to investigate foods, drugs, and restaurants; to segregate certain activities by zoning. All these have required government expenditures.

Income Growth. The growth in real per capita income is sometimes cited to explain the observed growth in government spending, for it is said that people demand disproportionately more government services as their incomes rise; that is, government services are said to have an income elasticity greater than one. This may be seen in the demand, in wealthy communities, for more expensive education programs (more specialized courses, more luxurious school facilities and furnishings, more costly equipment), larger budgets for libraries and cultural events, a higher level of services such as street repair and recreation programs, and a willingness to spend more for environmental protection.

The opposite phenomenon can also be observed. With more money, people become more independent of government services and less reliant on them. Instead of patronizing public swimming pools, they build their own. They use private automobiles instead of buses, and arrange for their own recreation by joining tennis and country clubs instead of lining up for public facilities. They buy books instead of borrowing them from libraries, and increase their personal security by installing alarms and locks and hiring guards. If they suspect the quality of their drinking water, they switch to bottled water.

From these contradictory factors Borcherding estimates that only about a fourth of the real increase in public spending in this century can be attributed to the increasing affluence of the populace.[4]

Redistribution. The areas of income security, welfare, health, housing, and education have been the principle loci of large and rapid government growth. But unlike public safety, water quality, and air traffic control, for example, there is little agreement about the extent to which government should supply or pay for such services. Scandalous abuse has gone hand in hand with new, humane programs. There is unemployment insurance for Vietnam war veterans, but also for school employees and forest rangers on seasonal vacations. There are health clinics for infants, but also assembly-line eye tests prescribed by unscrupulous doctors. There are classes for the handicapped, but also remedial reading courses in what are supposed to be universities. "There's a lot of money in poverty," however, much of it is said to go not to the deserving poor but to shady opportunists who operate will-o'-the wisp "nonprofit" neighborhood programs with unknown goals and dubious achievements.

The net effect of programs in these areas is to redistribute income, whether it is money per se that is being redistributed or the services that government pays for and distributes. Proponents of income redistribution view government as a mechanism readily at hand for performing this service. (Sometimes they seem oblivious to basic arithmetic, ignoring the indisputable fact that 10 percent of the population will inevitably be in the lowest income decile, except under ruthlessly perfect egalitarianism.)

Meltzer and Richard attribute much of the growth of government to the fact that the median voter has a median income, which is less than the average income; in other words, a majority of the voters have lower-than-average incomes. Therefore "those with the lowest income use the political process to increase their income. Politicians . . . attract voters with incomes near the median by offering benefits . . . that impose a net cost on those with incomes above the median."[5] This is especially feasible where taxation is progressive. The authors conclude their analysis on a somber note that government grows in every society where the majority remains free to express its will, despite the fact that large government is a threat to freedom.

This bleak forecast could be wrong, however. Perhaps the median voter doesn't vote. That is, while the median *eligible* voter earns less than an average income, the median *actual* voter may not. Voter turnout is embarrassingly low in the United States, and the poor are much less likely to vote than the wealthy. Furthermore, "one man, one vote" in no way means that every voter has the same degree of influence over public policy. The inexorable growth of government and the slide into totalitarianism or anarchy implied by Meltzer and Richard's voting analysis is not America's inevitable destiny.

Rectification of Societal Ills. Closely related to the foregoing explanation of government spending as a means to redistribute income is a broader pressure for government action to cure or at least ameliorate a wide variety of perceived shortcomings in society. There is a naive belief that government is omnipotent, that we know how to bring about desirable improvements, and that there exists a broad consensus as to what constitutes a desirable improvement in the first place.

Dissatisfaction with existing circumstances that were once accepted as an inevitable part of life brings forth a presumptuous effort to change those circumstances. As Wolf pointed out, rewards accrue in the political arena for publicizing problems and initiating programs that purport to solve them, however intractable the causes.[6] Thus the vainglorious attempt to provide normal lives for those with multiple handicaps, high-paying jobs for the unskilled, and a cure for cancer now. Unfortunately, not every deplorable condition succumbs to these government programs.

Fiscal Illusion. Fueling the increase in government spending is the illusion that government services are always a bargain. Clearly this is the case for every individual special-interest group, for its benefits are visible and individual, but the costs are diffuse and shared by all. It is only in the aggregate that the benefits are (at best) balanced by the costs, but unfortunately the aggregate has no identifiable constituency.

Contributing to this illusion is the simplistic notion that government doesn't make a profit, that all the inputs are transformed efficiently into outputs. One study of municipal services disproves this widely accepted but naive belief by demonstrating that the price charged by profit-making refuse-collection firms is actually substantially lower than the cost of non-profit municipal collection.[7]

Ordinary citizens are misled as to the cost of government. Surveys show that they consistently underestimate the amount of taxes they pay because of the ingenious "fiscal extraction devices" used by governments to raise revenues without the conscious knowledge of the taxpayer.[8] Property taxes are concealed in rents and mortgage payments. Sales taxes are collected by every retailer. No wonder the value-added tax is so attractive to elected officials.

The ultimate fiscal illusion may be found in the Soviet Union, where educated people will tell a foreign friend in all honesty that they pay little in the way of taxes and that only a very modest amount is withheld from their pay. A moment's reflection is needed to realize that when everyone is an employee of the state, all he knows is his take-home pay — he knows neither his true wages nor the amount withheld.

Even government officials are unaware of the cost of their services. Several studies found that the true costs of one municipal service in several cities were 30 percent greater on average than the amounts reported in the cities' budgets.[9]

The end result of fiscal illusion is pressure for government services in the belief that they are free, or nearly so, or at least an exceptional bargain.

Backlash. The foregoing factors and forces do not mean that the demand for more services is inevitable and ever increasing; government growth is not a one-way street. In cities with severe financial problems the size of municipal government has been cut in real terms. Throughout the country, Proposition 13 and its progeny burst upon the public policy scene as an antidote to demands for more government services. It seems as though the public, despairing of the ability or will of its elected government to reduce expenditures, has taken the matter directly into its hands and reduced revenue, like a parent rebuking his spendthrift child by cutting its allowance. President Reagan, giving effective voice to this same public mood and marshaling bipartisan support, drastically slashed both the federal budget and federal revenues, and put an end to "bracket creep" whereby tax collections rose more rapidly than inflation.

Increased Supply of Services

Whereas increased demand provides the "pull" for more government services, the desire by producers to supply more services provides a "push."

Political Imperatives. Elected officials gain considerable "political income" when government grows. From this point of view, it is far better to levy taxes and distribute them as subsidies to all than not to collect them, even though each individual citizen may be no better off. That is, an ideal program from a political viewpoint is one that extracts taxes as invisibly and painlessly as fiscal illusion can permit, and sends a check, signed by the elected official, individually to each citizen. The raising of revenue to be distributed is often hidden and diffuse, while the spending is frequently concentrated on particular, identifiable beneficiaries.

Ogden Nash expressed the point well in a delightful bit of doggerel entitled "The Politician":

> *He gains votes ever and anew*
> *By taking money from everybody and*
> *giving it to a few,*
> *While explaining that every penny*
> *Was extracted from the few to be given*
> *to the many*[10]

The institution of representative government itself facilitates this outcome. Individuals elect representatives and expect them to take care of government business on their behalf. Sensible individuals will then pay no attention to the details of government except for those few actions that affect them greatly.

Consider the hypothetical example of a complex bill that would reorganize a state university system. The promised educational benefits seem vague, but the financial consequences will be measurable: a tax increase of a dollar per year per capita and a raise of $500 per year for each professor. There is no rational reason why a voter would diligently apply himself to master the intricacies of the proposed legislation and to ferret out the fact that it would cost him a dollar. The average citizen knows little about the subject and is oblivious to the bill's consequences because they won't affect him. On the other hand, professors have the educational expertise to understand the bill, an incentive to do so, and an even stronger incentive to assure its passage. As Tullock points out, legislators know that this is how people behave and that by supporting the bill they are likely to get the votes of professors at the next election, while such action will have no effect on the votes of citizens who have no interest in the bill.[11] In short, politicians use public money to buy votes.

Congressmen earn electoral credits by establishing various federal programs, but in addition, "the legislation is drafted in very general terms, so some agency must translate a vague policy mandate into a functioning program, a process that necessitates the promulgation of rules and regulations. . . . At the next stage, aggrieved and/or hopeful constituents petition their Congressmen to intervene in the complex process of the bureaucracy. The cycle closes when the Congressman lends a sympathetic ear, piously denounces the evils of bureaucracy, intervenes in the latter's decisions, and rides a grateful electorate to ever more impressive electoral showings. Congressmen take credit coming and going."[12]

Larger government brings other political benefits. The office-holder can utilize his staff in his election campaigns. While technically illegal, this is a time-honored tradition that is widely observed and diligently followed. The larger the agency, the larger the campaign staff.

Budgetary Imperialism. Buchanan points indelicately to other incentives for growth that act on those within the government. More government work and more government expenditures inevitably mean more opportunities for larger salaries, higher status, more perquisites, and bigger bribes.[13] The larger the organization to be managed, and the greater the total resources under one's responsibility, the greater the salary. And along with a more imperial scope come suitably larger and nicer offices, a larger number of assistants and more attractive secretaries, car and chauffeur, plaques and photographs of handshaking on office walls, invitations to governors' mansions and the White House, and assorted other status symbols.

Staaf has demonstrated that consolidation of small school districts into larger ones results in more administrators per pupil and higher salaries for administrators and teachers.[14] (He further points out that in the absence of any proven relationship between educational inputs and outputs, the most likely effect of the *Serrano* v. *Priest* decision equalizing per pupil expenditures is to transfer income to teachers and administrators because education expenditures will rise in total.) The highest median income in the country is to be found in the environs of Washington, D.C., and the inflation of job titles and federal salaries has resulted in much higher pay in government than for corresponding work in the private sector.[15]

Budget maximization is the driving force in government agencies, and much of the observed growth can be attributed to this motivating principle, according to Niskanen.[16] He believes that bureaucrats take those actions that will maximize their budgets, and they do so not only for the pecuniary motives ascribed by Buchanan but also for nobler purposes that are directly in accord with what might be called the public interest. If a public official wants to change the thrust of his agency so that it will be more effective, it is much easier, quicker, and more painless to do so if the agency is expanding. To fire incompetents, change inherited attitudes, turn around a misguided unit, or galvanize a tired one into action is a lot harder than getting more money, creating a new unit, staffing it with fresh people, and setting it off with enthusiasm in a promising new direction. In short, even the most selfless public servant can honestly say that he is better able to serve the public interest if he has a bigger budget.

The Problem-Finding Elite. Another possible factor at work is the desire of an intellectual elite to gain power. According to Bethell,[17] our society has been producing a large number of educated people, and such people do relatively better in government than in the private sector. They are particularly adept at detecting societal ills, from rare occupational hazards to obscure but endangered fish species. They constitute a problem-finding elite whose numbers multiply as they seek more problems and offer their costly services to search for solutions.

Government Monopolies. Many government agencies are monopolies, in effect.[18] They find themselves in this enviable situation as a result of several contributing factors. In the first place, a principal function of government is to provide services that by their nature are monopolies or nearly so. Second, in the name of administrative efficiency and rational management, bureaus with partially overlapping functions have generally been combined, leaving the surviving agency with monopoly status. Third, at the local government level, the process of consolidation, school board mergers, annexation, creations of a regional government or authority, and city expansion to encompass previously unincorporated areas can result in the creation of an area-wide monopoly.[19]

Lacking competitors, a monopoly agency is inexorably driven to exercise its power and exploit its monolithically secure position. It does so in a variety of ways.

For one thing, its budget is particularly resistant to reduction. When asked to cut back on expenditures, it obediently presents a budget with the cuts focused on the most politically visible and popular programs, and when asked if the reductions couldn't be made in its other, less sensitive programs, it shrugs its shoulders helplessly. Its budget is often restored in short order.

One of the iniquitous practices of private monopolies is forcing consumers to purchase unwanted goods and services— "tie-in sales." If they don't buy these goods, they may not be permitted to buy the monopolized good they really want. Government monopolies behave no differently. Consider a city police department that says, in effect, "If you want uniformed police to do patrol work, you have to have uniformed police to answer the telephones and enforce parking regulations, too." Such a department resists creation of a separate, low-cost, specialized, civilian unit whose function is solely to enforce parking regulations. Its reasons for resistance include a desire to maximize both the number of police officers and the departmental budget, but also, it is sometimes whispered, to retain the power to extend courtesies to grateful offenders and police-fund contributors.

Should this illustration of governmental "tie-in sales" tactics strike one as far-fetched, note that the city of Plaquemine, Louisiana, tried to force some of its water customers to purchase city power as well. However, the U.S. Supreme Court sensibly ruled that the city is not automatically exempt from antitrust laws that prohibit such actions.[20]

The net effect of government's monopoly status is pressure for more government growth.

Employee Voting. For the aforementioned reasons, it is in the self-interest of public employees to have government grow. More than the average voter, therefore, they are motivated to vote, and to vote for candidates whose programs will enlarge government expenditures. After all, they are the most direct beneficiaries of government spending, except for citizens who receive direct transfer payments from government. Furthermore, they are numerically strong enough to affect the outcome of elections.

There is evidence to support the contention that government employees are more likely to vote and that their voting strength is significant. It is estimated from available data that public employees, who represent a sixth of the work force, cast more than a quarter of the votes.[21] The conventional wisdom in New York City is that municipal employees, each of whom can influence the votes of three relatives or friends, control a million votes, a number that greatly exceeds the margin of victory in any mayoral election.

The political power of public employees and their unions is not restricted to their voting strength. Political campaign contributions and campaign workers are a potent influence to which office seekers are surprisingly susceptible. The situation lends itself to collusion whereby officeholders can award substantial pay raises to employees with the unspoken understanding that some of the bread cast upon those particular waters will return as contributions; furthermore, a sudden increase in worker absenteeism during the campaign season might be conveniently overlooked by the city official who understands that the workers are temporarily engaged in a higher calling.

It was in recognition of this danger that the Hatch Act prohibited political activity by federal employees. There is no counterpart legislation at state or local levels, however, and the effectiveness of the Hatch Act is being undermined by court decisions. Similar considerations were no doubt responsible, at least in part, for denying the right to vote to residents of the District of Columbia, all of whom were presumed to be direct or indirect employees of the federal government.

Demand for Government Jobs. Not to be overlooked for its contribution to the growth of government is the simple demand for a government job. Perhaps the boldest expression of this occurred in New York City in the early 1970s, just before the fiscal symptoms of its managerial distress first surfaced. In response to an announcement of several hundred job openings for police officers, over one hundred thousand people applied for the civil service examination. (This is stunning evidence of the desirability of such jobs, but that is not the point here.) Tens of thousands passed the test, but, of course, relatively few were hired because of the city's limited need; the names of the others were put on the list of eligibles from which additional appointments might someday be made. What happened next was straight from the theater of the absurd: The people on the list formed an association, conducted demonstrations, and lobbied vigorously among city and state officials, demanding the enlargement of the police department and the appointment of more police officers.

Overproduction. Yet another factor on the supply side favoring government growth is the overproduction of services. This refers to the supply of more or better services than the public would willingly select if it had a direct choice and knew the true cost. In one commonplace public service, residential refuse collection, a detailed study shed light on this issue by examining the frequency of collection under circumstances where in some cities residents had both a greater choice of service level and more information about the cost of different service levels than in other cities.[22] Where a government agency

performed the work directly, or hired a private firm to do it at
direct government expense, collection was more frequent than
in cities where collection was mandatory but each household
made its own arrangement with a private firm and paid the latter directly for the service.

Inefficiency

A third major factor that accounts for the growth of government is growing inefficiency: spending more money and employing more people to do the same work.

Evidence can readily be found in New York City, not because it is worse than other governments, but, on the contrary,
because it is relatively open to scrutiny. Perhaps the most re-
markable statistic is drawn from the police department: Over
a twenty-five-year period the number of police officers rose
from 16,000 to 24,000, but the total annual hours worked by
the entire force actually declined slightly. The entire 50 percent
increase in manpower was completely devoted to shortening
the workweek, lengthening the lunch hour and vacation period, and providing more holidays and paid sick leave.

Inefficient staffing was legitimized by a state law that called
for an equal number of police officers on duty on each shift,
despite the fact that crime statistics showed few criminals
working in the small hours of the morning. Because of this leg-
islated inefficiency, if more police were needed for assignment
to evening duty, when most street crimes occur, more would
also have to be hired and assigned when there was little or no
work for them to do.

Growing inefficiency is also evident in publicly operated
mass transit. Because the great preponderance of passenger
trips occur during rush hours, few bus drivers are needed between those two periods. "Split-shift" scheduling using part-
time drivers makes obvious sense; instead, some drivers for the
New York Metropolitan Transportation Authority drive a to-

tal of eight hours a day but are also paid (at overtime rates) for a four-hour Mediterranean-style break at midday.

In the New York City school system, during a period of constant pupil enrollment, a 50 percent increase in the number of teachers and the addition of one paraprofessional for every two teachers produced only a slight decrease in class size. Instead, classroom time was reduced for teachers, and some teacher duties were delegated to the paraprofessionals. It is by no means obvious that the result was better teacher preparation and better pupil education.

A careful study of the growth of New York City expenditures for health, education, and welfare concluded that enormous additional sums were spent on higher real salaries and more jobs without evidence of increased outputs or higher quality of services.[23] Spann examined labor-to-output ratios for several public services during a period in the mid-1960s and concluded that average productivity was either unchanged or declined for state and local government employees.[24] Thus, while inefficiency is not restricted to government activity, declining productivity and increasing inefficiency in government help explain the growth in the size and cost of government.

CONCLUSION

There are strong and undeniable pressures for government to grow in response to public demands, in response to the desires of service producers to supply more services, and as a consequence of inefficiency. If unchecked, these factors would lead to an unstable and uncontrollable spiral of continued growth: the bigger the government, the greater the force for even bigger government. Budgets will expand, resulting in the appointment of more officials and the hiring of more workers. These will go to work at once to enlarge their budgets, do less work, hire still more workers, obtain better-than-average raises, and vote for more spending programs, while encouraging their constituents and beneficiaries to do the same. The forecast seems ominous: Sooner or later everyone will be working for government.

But simple extrapolations of this sort are not correct. Countervailing homeostatic forces come into play from time to time, as in the taxpayer revolt symbolized by Proposition 13, in state-mandated "caps" on local expenditures, and in proposals for a constitutional amendment requiring a balanced budget. Political leaders find that they can gain more support by cutting back on spending programs than by initiating new ones. Revenue cuts and revenue limitations are politically popular. Voters reject spending proposals, elect more frugal officials, and flee from high-tax jurisdictions. President Carter was elected in part because of his *non*-Washington background; President Reagan was elected in great measure because of his *anti*-Washington stance: Get the government off the backs of the people.

Furthermore, public employees are not united in a headless conspiracy; they feel just as victimized as other taxpayers when they receive poor and costly services in return for their tax dollars: Proposition 13 was supported by 44 percent of families that included public employees.[25] Under budgetary stringency, the objectives of one government bureau are at odds with those of another, and instead of making common cause to enlarge their total budget, they fight each other to obtain a larger share of the pie.

A more educated, critical, and sophisticated citizenry no longer regards government action as synonymous with the public interest. It is learning to expect unintended, adverse consequences of attempts at social engineering, and it recognizes limits in the state's ability to define — let alone attain — the public good.

NOTES

1. Peter F. Drucker, *Saturday Review,* April 1973, p. 41.
2. "Washington's New Growth Industry," *Public Interest,* no. 56 (Summer 1979): 116.
3. Charles Brecher, *Where Have All the Dollars Gone?* (New York: Praeger, 1974), p. 94.
4. Thomas E. Borcherding, ed., *Budgets and Bureaucrats: The Sources of Government Growth* (Durham, N.C.: Duke University Press, 1977), p. 50.
5. Allan H. Meltzer and Scott F. Richard, "Why Government Grows (and Grows) in a Democracy," *Public Interest,* no. 52 (Summer 1978): 111-18.
6. Charles Wolf, Jr., "A Theory of Non-market Failure," *Public Interest,* no. 55 (Spring 1979): 114-33.
7. E.S. Savas, "Public vs. Private Refuse Collection: A Critical Review of the Evidence," *Journal of Urban Analysis* 6 (1979): 1-13.
8. Richard E. Wagner, "Revenue Structure, Fiscal Illusion, and Budgetary Choice," *Public Choice* 25 (Spring 1976): 45-61. Also, James M. Buchanan, "Why Does Government Grow?" in Borcherding, *Budgets and Bureaucrats.*
9. E.S. Savas, "How Much Do Government Services Really Cost?" *Urban Affairs Quarterly* 15 (September 1979): 23-42.
10. Ogden Nash, *I'm a Stranger Here Myself* (Boston: Little, Brown, 1938), p. 193.
11. Gordon Tullock, "Why Politicians Won't Cut Taxes," *Taxing and Spending,* October/November 1978, pp. 12-14.
12. Morris P. Fiorina, *Congress: Keystone of the Washington Establishment* (New Haven: Yale University Press, 1977).
13. Buchanan, "Why Does Government Grow?" p. 13.
14. Robert J. Staaf, "The Public School System in Transition: Consolidation and Parental Choice," in Borcherding, *Budgets and Bureaucrats,* pp. 143-46.
15. Tom Bethell, "The Wealth of Washington," *Harper's Magazine,* June 1978, pp. 41-60.
16. William A. Niskanen, Jr., *Bureaucracy and Representative Government* (Chicago: Aldine-Atherton, 1971), pp. 36-42.
17. Bethell, "The Wealth of Washington."
18. E.S. Savas, "Municipal Monopoly," *Harper's Magazine,* December 1971, pp. 55-60.

19. Robert L. Bish and Robert Warren, "Scale and Monopoly Problems in Urban Government Services," *Urban Affairs Quarterly* 8 (September 1972): 97-122.

20. 435 U.S. 389 (1978).

21. Thomas E. Borcherding, Winston C. Bush, and Robert M. Spann, "The Effects on Public Spending of the Divisibility of Public Outputs in Consumption, Bureaucratic Power, and the Size of the Tax-Sharing Group," in Borcherding, *Budgets and Bureaucrats,* p. 219.

22. E.S. Savas, *The Organization and Efficiency of Solid Waste Collection* (Lexington, Mass.: Lexington Books, 1977), pp. 67-78.

23. Brecher, *Where Have All the Dollars Gone?* p. 99.

24. Robert M. Spann, "Rates of Productivity Change and the Growth of State and Local Governmental Expenditures," in Borcherding, *Budgets and Bureaucrats,* pp. 100-129.

25. Jacob Citrin, "The Alienated Voter," *Taxing and Spending,* October/November 1978.

CHAPTER 3

THE NATURE OF GOODS AND SERVICES

To understand how a more limited, modest, and sensible role for government might be realized, let us begin at the beginning by looking at the different kinds of goods and services that people need and then let us examine the appropriate nature of government involvement in the process of satisfying those needs.

Human beings require many different kinds of goods and services. Food, clothing, and shelter are the basic necessities of life, but unless one is a hermit, additional goods and services are necessary. For example, even primitive tribes seek protection from human enemies and assistance from divine beings, and therefore they support warriors and weapon makers to provide the former and priests and shamans to provide the latter services.

In more complex societies with highly specialized division of labor, the list of needed goods and services is virtually endless: fire protection and banking services, old-age security, transportation and communication, recreation, health care and waste removal, theaters and cemeteries, museums and beauty parlors, landscaping and tailoring, books and locks, money and water. The classified section of the local telephone directory is a condensed catalog of the goods and services required in an industrial, urbanized society.

An examination of the basic characteristics of these and other goods and services reveals that certain kinds of goods have special attributes that require some sort of collective action. To start this inquiry it is useful to classify this vast jumble of goods and services not in alphabetical order, as in the Yellow Pages, but according to two important concepts: exclusion and joint consumption.[1]

EXCLUSION

Goods and services—henceforth these terms will be used synonymously, for the distinction between goods and services is not important in this discussion—have the characteristic of exclusion if the potential user of the goods can be denied the goods or excluded from their use unless he meets the conditions set by the potential supplier. In other words, the goods can change hands only if both the buyer and seller agree on the terms.

Now this is a perfectly ordinary sort of condition. All the commonplace goods and services that we buy in the marketplace clearly fall into this category; all have this exclusion property. I may walk off with my bag of groceries only after my grocer agrees. (We can ignore the possibility of theft—we know it occurs, but it is not germane to the discussion.) But there are vast numbers of other goods and services that do *not* possess this simple property. A consumer can simply help himself to such goods as long as Mother Nature or another supplier make them available. As one example of such a good, consider a lighthouse. Built at considerable expense on a rocky coast, and consuming large amounts of costly energy, the lighthouse sends forth its beacon to help seamen navigate the treacherous waters in its vicinity. This is a valuable service for the seafarer, but he does not pay the lighthouse keeper for it; he can avail himself of it freely and cannot be excluded from doing so. After all, what is the keeper to do? Turn off the beacon when he knows that this particular nonpaying user is in the area?[2]

The water of a large freshwater lake is another example of a good whose consumption cannot conveniently be prevented or excluded. Consumers can drink freely of the water, and can use it for irrigation purposes without paying anyone for its use.

It should be recognized that exclusion is a matter of cost more than logic; exclusion is feasible or infeasible to the extent that the cost of effecting or enforcing exclusion is relatively low or high. Hence, exclusion admits of degrees. Exclusion from the services of a lighthouse is rather infeasible; exclusion in the purchase of goods from a store is easily feasible. But other goods cannot be allocated quite so neatly into the feasible and infeasible categories with respect to exclusion. For example, it is feasible to charge admission (and therefore to practice exclusion) for a grandstand seat to a fireworks display, but many others outside the grounds will also see the show, although perhaps not as well as those in the seats. It is simply not feasible to enclose a large enough area so that no one can witness the show free of charge—unless the show is a poor one with no high-altitude bursts.

Joint Consumption

The other important characteristic of goods and services that is relevant to this discussion has to do with consumption. Some goods may be used or consumed jointly and simultaneously by many customers without being diminished in quality or quantity, while other goods are available only for individual (rather than joint) consumption; that is, if they are used by one consumer, they are not available for consumption by another. A fish and a haircut are examples of a good and a service subject to individual consumption; the fish is no longer available to another angler or diner, and neither are the services of the barber while he is cutting someone's hair. (Other, comparable barbers may be available to others in need of tonsorial attention—just as similar fish are available to other anglers and diners—and the very same chair and barber will be available in a few minutes, but the fact remains that the services of that particular barber at that particular time are devoted to and consumed entirely by the one user.)

Contrast these cases with a television broadcast. My family's "consumption" of a program, by enjoying it on our television set in our living room, in no way limits its "consumption" by anyone else, or even by millions of other viewers who may turn on their sets. The program remains equally available for joint consumption by many users and is in no way diminished or made less useful by our act of consumption.

One should not be confused by the fact that the fish may be fed to several people at a dinner party; that act does not confer upon the fish the property of joint consumption, in the rigorous sense in which we have used that term here. Similarly, my solitary viewing of a TV show does not transform that telecast into an individually consumed good.

Another illustration of a joint-consumption good is national defense. National defense is a joint-consumption good. The protection I receive from the armed forces in no way subtracts from the protection available to my neighbor; his consumption of that particular good is undiminished by my own. (Of course, some would argue that the existence of armed forces is a *threat* to their personal security, but that is because different people value the same goods and services differently.)

Other examples of goods that are subject to joint consumption are parks and streets. One person's use of Grand Canyon National Park does not preclude another's use of it; it is a jointly consumed good, as is a city street. In both cases, however, it is recognized that if the total number of joint users is large relative to the capacity of the park or street, then the quantity and quality of the available goods become severely diminished. In other words, these goods—parks and streets—are not *pure* joint-consumption goods like the TV broadcast.

To a degree, they partake of the characteristics of a haircut, an individually consumed good. In fact, no goods are pure joint-consumption goods; they fall along a continuum between pure individual and pure joint consumption.

CLASSIFYING GOODS AND SERVICES

What has been said so far can be displayed in the form of a diagram, as in figure 3.1 on page 34. The two properties, exclusion and jointness of consumption, constitute the two dimensions of the diagram and are shown as continuous variables; the pure forms correspond to the ends of the scales. Several illustrative goods and services are listed within the boundaries of the diagram, located in accordance with their respective degrees of exclusion and joint consumption. (Obviously, there is subjective judgment involved in the precise placement of services in this diagram.)

The four corners of the diagram correspond to pure forms: (1) pure individually consumed goods for which exclusion is completely feasible; (2) pure jointly consumed goods for which exclusion is completely feasible; (3) pure individually consumed goods for which exclusion is completely infeasible; (4) pure jointly consumed goods for which exclusion is completely infeasible. These four idealized types of goods and services are important enough and will be referred to often enough to justify naming them; this has been done in the diagram. In the sequence listed above, they are called respectively (1) private goods, (2) toll goods, (3) common-pool goods, and (4) collective goods.

The reason for classifying goods in this manner is that the nature of the good determines whether or not it will be produced at all, and the conditions needed to assure that it will be supplied. Private goods are consumed individually and cannot be obtained by the user without the assent of the supplier, which is usually obtained by making payment. Common-pool

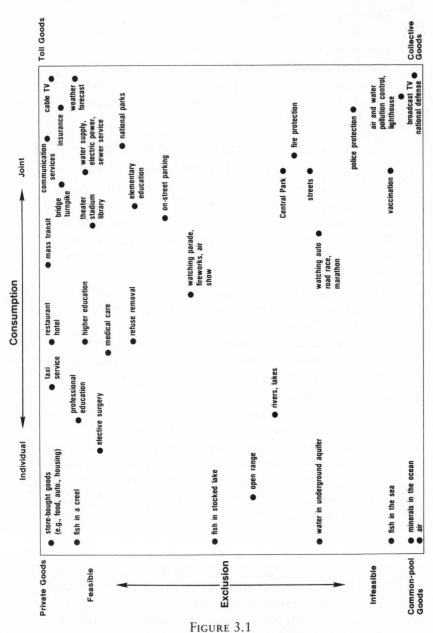

FIGURE 3.1

Diagram showing the exclusion and joint-consumption properties of various goods and services. Pure goods are shown at the four corner points.

goods are consumed individually, and it is virtually impossible to prevent anyone from taking them freely. Toll goods are used jointly, but the users must pay, and those who won't pay can easily be excluded from enjoying the use of the goods. The more difficult or costly it is to exclude a consumer from the use of a toll good, the more like a collective good it is. Collective goods are used jointly, and it is impossible to exclude anyone from their use, which means that people generally will not pay for them without coercion. This important discussion of the relation between the nature of the good and how to assure an adequate supply of the good will be resumed more fully after reviewing and classifying some of the principal goods used in a modern society.

The goods that appear in the diagram near the corners can be considered private goods, toll goods, common-pool goods, or collective goods, although it should be remembered that none of them are pure or ideal types. In the upper left of the diagram appear the ordinary goods and services that one buys in the marketplace: shoes, bread, automobiles, housing, haircuts, dry cleaning, watch repair, etc. They are all pure or nearly pure private goods.

In the lower right of the diagram are collective goods. Air pollution control is as pure a collective good as one can find. National defense is a collective good, but even this is impure: An army busy defending one part of the country may be unavailable to protect another part. Police protection is almost as pure a collective good, but any finite force on patrol can be "consumed" by individual calls for service, making the good temporarily unavailable to others. For this reason it is shown above and to the left of national defense. On the other hand, fire protection used to be a toll good or even a somewhat private good, for it was common in the nineteenth century to have private fire companies that protected only their paying subscribers, whose homes were marked with identifying placards. Today, however, particularly in urban areas, we recognize that when a house is on fire, many people besides the homeowner benefit by having the blaze extinguished before it spreads. Furthermore, it is no longer technically feasible to exclude service in densely packed, high-rise, multiple dwellings. Fire protection has migrated into the class of collective goods.

Central Park in New York City was also a toll good when it was first built. It has a wall around it, pierced by many gates that were once tended by gatekeepers who charged admission. The wall and gates are still there, but the gatekeepers have long since gone, exclusion is no longer practiced, and the park is used—and abused—as a collective good. National parks have limited access points and are therefore toll goods, but a determined backpacker can hike into one through the wilderness and, realistically, cannot be excluded. Because the quality of a park depends on the number of users and the uses they make of it, parks are shown as being more individually consumed than some other toll and collective goods.

Air is a common-pool good. It can be used and taken freely and compressed, but upon compression it is changed into a purely private good. It can also be used and soiled, thereby rendering it unavailable to others in its original condition. Similarly, a fish in the sea is a common-pool good, and a fish in a stocked lake is somewhere between a common-pool good and private good (the lake could be patroled and only those who purchase a license granted access to the fish), but once a fish is caught and in the creel, it is clearly a private good.

Water in an underground aquifer is a common-pool good, free to be tapped by any well digger who owns a tiny parcel of land above it, but once it is brought into a water distribution system, it becomes a toll good. Rivers, lakes, and other waterways are common-pool goods of sorts, whether they are used for transportation, as sources of water, or to dispose of waste material. As figure 3.1 shows, they are decidedly impure common-pool goods because exclusion is by no means impossible.

Telephone service is a toll good whose quality is actually enhanced when other users consume it jointly: the more participants, the broader the reach of the communication network. The same is true of postal and telegraph services and insurance.

Sewer service and electric power are toll goods, as are bridges, turnpikes, stadiums, theaters, and libraries, although none of these is as pure a toll good as cable TV or a weather forecast prepared by a private weather service for its clients. Even broadcast television becomes a toll good if receivers must be licensed, as is the case in some countries.

While mass transit is a toll good, taxi service is more of a private good, and a private automobile is a more purely private good. In general, on-street parking is a collective good, although where there are parking meters it has been made into a toll good that is impure insofar as it has limited capacity. Streets are a collective good, for it is difficult to exclude the use of a street for passage; that is, it is costly to construct and to man barriers.

To exclude someone from a school is not difficult, but at least an elementary education can be obtained without formal schooling. Furthermore, particularly with elementary education, joint consumption occurs to some degree. The relative positions of elementary and higher education are displayed on the diagram of figure 3.1. As the *Bakke* case showed, accepting one applicant into medical school means rejecting another, and therefore the higher the level of education under consideration, the more the service resembles a private good.

Health care presents an interesting case that cannot be analyzed without considering separate portions of the health-care system. Elective and cosmetic surgery, treatment for vitamin deficiencies and metabolic disorders, and medical care after accidental injury are private goods. Public health services such as mosquito abatement, rat control, and immigration control to prevent the importation of contagious diseases are obviously collective goods. Immunization and treatment for communicable diseases, whether sore throats or diphtheria, at first glance seem to satisfy all the criteria of private goods. A person with such an illness can certainly be denied treatment, and, if admitted to a hospital, the bed he occupies and the nursing and medical care he receives are no longer available to others. However, it is evident that treating such illnesses provides important side benefits—"positive externalities"—in that others are not exposed to the illnesses. Therefore, many people receive benefits, or partake of the fruits of this particular good, at the same time as the patient and without reducing the latter's benefits. Going back to the elective surgery mentioned above, this service, too, can benefit others, if the patient is better able to work and support his family and provide employment to his workers. Clearly, however, except for the aforementioned public health measures, health care has the exclusion property and falls somewhere within the range of private and toll goods.

This lengthy exercise in classifying goods and services has made it clear that the nature of the good—private, toll, common-pool, or collective—determines the willingness of producers to supply it and consumers to pay for it, and therefore affects whether or not collective intervention is needed to procure the good in satisfactory quantity and quality. The next several sections explore this issue for each type of good.

Private Goods

Private goods pose no conceptual problem of supply; the marketplace provides them. Consumers demand the goods; entrepreneurs recognize the demand, produce the goods, and sell them to willing buyers at a mutually satisfactory price. Collective action with respect to private goods for the most part is confined to assuring their safety (e.g., of food, drugs, elevators, buildings), honest reporting (of weights and measures, interest rates, labels), and the like. Of course, no one will be able to secure all the private goods he may deserve, and some may to be too poor to afford even the rudimentary necessities without financial assistance.

COMMON-POOL GOODS

Common-pool goods do pose a supply problem. With no need to pay for such goods, and with no means to prevent their consumption, such goods will be consumed — even squandered — to the point of exhaustion, as long as the cost of collecting, harvesting, extracting, appropriating, or otherwise taking direct possession of the free goods does not exceed the value of the goods to the consumer. It would appear at first glance that no rational supplier would produce such goods, and they would exist only through the beneficence of nature. We will see later that this is not necessarily the case.

Whales, tigers, and elephants are living — or rather dying — proof of the problem of managing common-pool goods that belong to whoever takes them. They are being consumed to the point of extinction, despite the fact that these are naturally renewable goods.

Market mechanisms fail to assure a continued supply of common-pool goods. Instead, other forms of collective or cooperative actions are required. In the case of whales and animals, this takes the form of international efforts to achieve voluntary agreement among the consumers to limit their consumption. (This is also true of Antarctica, currently a common-pool good.) This has proven to be a thin reed to support such a burden, however, as enforcement is next to impossible. Another approach is to ban the sale of common-pool goods after they are taken and transformed into private goods. (Not all common-pool goods lend themselves to this approach.) Following this tactic, in the United States the sale of products made of alligator hides, tiger skins, ostrich feathers, or other endangered species is prohibited; and in Kenya the government tries to prohibit the sale of elephant tusks and rhinoceros horns. This approach, too, has had limited success. Note that the commissions, agencies, regulatory bodies, and enforcement units created to deal with the problem of common-pool goods are providing a service that is, in effect, a collective good.

Just as whales and tigers have been appropriated from the common pool and transformed into private goods, some rivers and lakes represent common-pool goods that have been used freely as dumps for toxic and noxious wastes and therefore have been debased into lower-quality, less available, partly consumed private goods. This destruction of common-pool goods, the pollution of waterways, has also called forth collective action. Government controls have been established over sources of pollution such as industrial plants and sewage treatment facilities. In effect, a new service is provided, water pollution control (a collective good), in order to assure a continued supply of the desired common-pool good — unpolluted waterways.

The moon is a far-out example of a common-pool good. It could be used as a source of raw materials or as a communication or military base, but it is at least temporarily protected from overconsumption because of the high cost of using it. Nevertheless, outer space is already being degraded as a common-pool good as more and more waste products from space explorations orbit the Earth.

When the common-pool good in question comes under the jurisdiction of a single organization, whether a sovereign government or a private monopolist, successful management is more likely than when the good in question involves more than one organization. Fishing restrictions within the United States are more effective than whale-catch limits in the oceans, and an underground oil deposit whose drilling rights belong to a single producer can be managed more effectively than one that can be tapped from dozens of overlying parcels of land. That is because the deposit is no longer a common-pool good; it has been acquired in toto and transformed into a private good, as is the case with a private lake, for example.

These few examples illustrate the problems inherent in supplying common-pool goods: the danger of depletion, the need for collective action, the creation of collective services (usually provided by government regulatory agencies) to safeguard the goods, and the limited effectiveness of such regulation because exclusion is difficult to achieve.

TOLL GOODS

Unlike common-pool goods, toll goods can be supplied by the marketplace. Because exclusion is readily possible, users will pay and therefore suppliers will supply the goods, theoretically in the quantity and quality demanded by the users. Nevertheless, toll goods present problems that require collective action. Many toll goods are natural monopolies, which is to say that as the number of users increases, the cost per user decreases. This is true of cable television, communication networks, and utilities such as electric power, gas distribution, water supply, and sewer service. Collective action may be required to assure that these monopolies are created and granted in the first place and then regulated so that the owners do not exploit their monopoly privileges unfairly.

It is worth remarking that many toll goods are no longer monopolies even though they once were. Railroads face competition from airplanes, trucks and buses, and barges and boats. Telephone communication is challenged by microwave and facsimile transmission, and television broadcasting by cable TV and videotaped programming.

COLLECTIVE GOODS

It is collective goods that pose a serious problem in the organization of a society. The marketplace is unable to supply such goods because, by their nature, they are used simultaneously by many people and no one can be excluded from enjoying them. An individual has an economic incentive to make full use of such goods without paying for them and without contributing a fair share of the effort required to supply them, that is, to become a "free rider." Aristotle said it long ago: "That which is common to the greatest number has the least care bestowed upon it." If no one volunteers to pay for such goods, surely no one will volunteer to produce them, at least not in adequate supply. Therefore, collective contributions—usually taxes—have to be obtained in order to assure a supply of the goods. In small groups, social pressures may be sufficient to assure that each person contributes his or her fair share to secure the collective goods, but in larger, more diverse groups, legally sanctioned coercion is necessary.

Measuring and Choosing Collective Goods

Collective goods have other properties that exacerbate the already serious consequences of their joint-consumption and nonexcludable characteristics. They are generally hard to measure and they offer little choice to the consumer.

Unlike private goods, which are relatively easy to count, account for, and package for unit sales, collective goods generally do not permit of such ease in handling. How many units of national defense should be purchased? How much police protection? One can count the number of firemen in a fire department, but that number offers no reliable measure of the amount of fire protection they provide. One can report the area of a park, but that says little about it; appearance and ambience are inherent aspects of that particular good. Street mileage can be measured and traffic and potholes can be counted, but these hard facts barely begin to capture the important features of that particular collective good. The product of an air pollution control department can be measured only indirectly, in terms of air quality, and even that is subject to extraneous factors, such as a strong breeze. For these reasons, it is difficult — but by no means impossible — to define and measure the performance of an organization charged with providing a collective good. And this difficulty means that it is difficult to specify the amount of the good to be provided and to estimate what it should cost.

The very nature of a collective good means that an individual has little choice with respect to consuming the good, and he must generally accept it in the quantity and quality available. The ordinary citizen can demand that a policeman be stationed in front of his home, that his street be swept daily, and that his neighborhood park look like a royal garden; but his voice is diluted, and although his taxes may rise, the collective goods he receives are not likely to change much. Neither the individual who feels that the country is in danger and needs more military might nor the individual who feels that the nation's security is threatened by too much military power in the hands of fallible mortals will be satisfied, for he has no individual choice in the matter. He may lobby his congressman, but must settle for what he can get.

A further consequence of these characteristics is that because it is impossible to charge directly for the use of collective goods, payment for them is unrelated to demand or consumption. Therefore, instead of relying on a market mechanism, one must rely on a political process to decide how much each user must pay, and whether or not some users are to receive a discount. Furthermore, to the extent that most collective goods are impure, and admit of individual consumption to some degree, the decision as to who gets them is also relegated to the political process.

At this point it is worth reviewing and summarizing the important differences between private and collective goods, in

order to appreciate better the profound nature of the differences; this is done in table 3.1.

TABLE 3.1
Comparison of Private and Collective Goods

Characteristic	Private Good	Collective Good
Consumption	Entirely by an individual	Joint and simultaneous by many people
Payment for goods	Related to consumption; paid by consumer	Unrelated to consumption; paid by collective contributions
Exclusion of someone who will not pay	Easy	Difficult
Measurement of quantity and quality of goods	Easy	Difficult
Measurement of performance of goods producer	Easy	Difficult
Individual choice in consuming or not	Yes	No
Individual choice as to quantity and quality of goods consumed	Yes	No
Allocation decisions	Made by market mechanism	Made by political process

THE INCREASE IN COLLECTIVE
AND COMMON-POOL GOODS

The problem of providing collective goods is compounded further by the fact that the number of such goods is growing. The
number is growing for three reasons. First, they are being
created by the need to husband common-pool goods whose
scarcity has only recently been recognized. As we have seen,
pollution control and the negotiation and enforcement of international agreements are examples of such newly created
collective goods.

Second, individuals can and do create collective goods by
transforming their private goods, thereby shifting the burden

of payment on to collective shoulders. For example, the person who throws his garbage into the street instead of subscribing to a refuse-collection service eschews the private good and creates a need for the collective good called street cleaning.

Third, many goods have migrated out of the private and toll-good classes and into the class of collective goods. Such migrations or transformations result from changed conditions, as exemplified by the movement of fire protection from toll good to collective good, from political decisions that certain goods are so worthy that consumption is to be encouraged regardless of ability to pay, and from changing knowledge and attitudes about positive and negative side effects.

The collective political decision to supply and encourage the consumption of certain worthy goods regardless of the consumer's willingness or ability to pay results in subsidies to private enterprises or direct production of service by an agency of the collective will, which may be a government bureau or quasi-government authority. Examples abound: Recreation services that are toll goods according to our definition are given away free of charge to the user. Bridges, turnpikes, mass transit, and other transportation services are often subsidized. Theaters, concert halls, opera houses, sports arenas, stadiums, museums, and exhibition halls are often built with public funds and receive operating subsidies as well.

The straightforward toll goods of electric, gas, and telephone service may be in the early stages of being similarly redefined. For example, a demand that they be provided without charge under certain circumstances, hence rendering them indistinguishable in practice from collective goods, arose following a particularly tragic incident in New England one recent winter when an elderly couple, incapable of caring for themselves yet living alone, had their utilities unwittingly turned off for nonpayment of bills and consequently froze to death.

If no use is made of the exclusion property of toll goods, that is, if there is little or no charge for their use, then in effect the good is transformed into a collective good. This occurs by political decision. In terms of the diagram of goods and their attributes, figure 3.1, a toll good given away without charge drops down vertically to the line of no exclusion and must be provided or paid for by collective contributions, either voluntary donations or tax levies. (A good that is partially subsidized drops part way to that line.)

Side effects, or externalities, abound in an urban society. Everything is connected to everything else, and some goods spill over and affect others. Refuse removal may be almost a pure private good in a rural setting, but in a city it is more of a toll good, and one that may even be worth subsidizing or giving away and thus being redefined and treated as a collective good; after all, I, too, will benefit if my neighbor has his refuse collected regularly, and I will suffer if he does not.

A minor but nevertheless interesting example of redefining the nature of a good occurred recently. As we've said, a fish in the sea is a prototypical example of a common-pool good. Indeed, until 1977 the fish outside the 12-mile limit in international waters off the New England coast were so regarded. Then the United States in effect appropriated these fish for its citizens, and redefined them to be collective goods, by extending to 200 miles the limits of its territorial waters and sending the Coast Guard to watch over them. (In reality, of course, it was a side effect — the well-being of the local fishing industry — that was deemed to be a collective good. This particular collective action and the political side benefits appurtenant thereto illustrate why and how government grows.)

Changes in societal values have brought about redefinition or reclassification of goods. Not so long ago education was regarded as a private good. Exclusion and individual consumption were clearly identifiable attributes of this good. An education bestowed great and obvious benefits to the recipient, and this much-prized good was sought and sold in the marketplace. In time, however, a new perception arose. It was that the entire society benefited significantly if everyone was educated, much like vaccination; education was considered to have major, positive side effects associated with it, and therefore its consumption was to be made available to all and subsidized or given away. In short, exclusion was barred; education was displaced vertically downward in figure 3.1, where, somewhat like air, it became freely available to all. In fact, consumption of at least a minimum amount of education is compulsory in most developed societies. This minimum level has been increasing in the United States, and higher education seems to be following the same migratory path in the goods diagram as did elementary education. The growing insistence that medical doctors are a national resource suggests that medical schools will follow the same route.

An even better example of reclassification caused by changing social values is the most basic good: eating food. How could there be a purer private good? Nevertheless, the inevitable consequence of treating food as a purely private good is the appearance of starving beggars in the streets. Not only starving beggars but also well-fed humanitarians will enjoy the side benefits of collective action taken to distribute food to the poor. One doesn't have to travel to Calcutta to conclude that food stamps, besides appealing to one's humane instincts, beautify the urban landscape as well.

The example of housing parallels that of food; while this, too, is a seemingly private good, redefinition has taken place, externalities have been discovered, and as a result public housing has been subsidized for a large class of eligible consumers. It is asserted that everyone benefits by demolishing slums and providing decent housing to former slum dwellers at collective expense.

At the extreme, one can claim that any good has some joint-consumption character by saying that a citizen who lacks a particular private good, and therefore has an unfulfilled need, will become disaffected from the larger society; this in turn will lead to social instability, which threatens everyone. By this reasoning, all private goods have side benefits that benefit everyone in the society at large and hence should be provided at collective expense.

Such actions have unfortunate consequences, however. As has been said, all goods are somewhat subject to individual consumption, for there are no pure joint-consumption goods. When subsidized, underpriced, or given away without charge, the demand for the good increases. As a result, the available supplies are consumed, and public expenditures must be made to supply enough of these goods. What has happened is that many subsidized services have become common-pool goods, in effect, and are subject to all the problems inherent in such goods: rampant waste, thoughtless consumption, and possible exhaustion. To the extent that the handling of "junk mail" is underpriced, postal service is an example of an impure toll good that has tended to become a casually consumed, exhaustible, common-pool good. Unmetered municipal water is another case in point. Anyone associated with the free lunch programs in schools is keenly aware of the prodigious waste that occurs, and scandals associated with free summer lunch programs in large cities reveal the same thing: large amounts of food treated as a worthless good and discarded. Public schooling is treated in much the same way by many careless consumers.

The recent experience with medical care in the United States offers an even more dramatic illustration of a redefined good. As was discussed above, most medical care could be characterized as an individually consumed good readily subject to exclusion, that is, a private good. However, a gradual change in societal values led to the recognition, determination, or compassionate belief that individual medical care has joint-consumption properties: A lot of people feel better when a sick person is cured. Thus, medical care was subsidized or provided at nominal or no charge as a result of various collective decisions embodied in legislation. What happened next was an explosion of demand, a proliferation of multiple visits to greedy doctors in "Medicaid mills," and a large increase in unnecessary laboratory tests, hospital admissions, and surgical procedures. Thus, to a significant degree, medical care has become a common-pool good, there for the taking like the fish in the sea, but even more accessible. One can predict with confidence the creation of commissions to investigate, and agencies to attempt to control, the waste and high cost involved in providing this low-cost (to the consumer) common-pool good.

One can postulate the general rule that private goods and impure toll goods subsidized to a significant degree or provided without a user charge—that is, goods whose exclusion property is abandoned—will be transformed into common-pool goods, subject to all the problems of such goods. The only restraints to infinite consumption of such goods are their exhaustion and the cost of taking the goods. In the case of medical care, it is the nurses, doctors, and hospital beds that can be exhausted, and it is the fuss and bother of making appointments, waiting in lines, and filling out reimbursement claims that constitute the cost of taking the toll-free goods.

For a final example of reclassified goods, witness the collective action of the New York State Legislature in 1977: It decreed that all pay toilets in the state shall henceforth be free. In other words, a new common-pool good was created by fiat, and the consequences can be foreseen: the gradual disappearance of public toilets and either government construction and operation of public toilets, as in many European cities, or legislation requiring various businesses to maintain public toilets as an ancillary service, which will result in higher prices for the primary goods provided by those businesses.

It should also be noted in passing that some collective goods can be replaced, in part at least, by private goods. Locks, burglar alarms, karate lessons, smoke alarms, home fire extinguishers, and automatic fire sprinklers are examples of private goods being used increasingly as partial substitutes for the collective goods of police and fire protection. Furthermore, a very wealthy person could transform collective goods into private goods by having his own guards, a large estate with private roads, and private park and gardens, as at Versailles. Given sufficient incentive, more metering and exclusion devices could be invented that would make it possible to transform other collective goods into toll or private goods; for example, autos could be charged for the use of particular city streets during congested periods, as advocated by Vickrey.[3]

Nevertheless, in the main, it is private goods that have been undergoing reclassification as common-pool goods, and toll goods have been subsidized or provided free so that they resemble collective goods. Evidence is provided by the changing allocation of government expenditures. Spending for health, education, income maintenance, and housing—all of which are predominantly private and toll goods, as we have seen—grew dramatically in twenty-five years and now constitutes almost half the federal budget, up from an eighth. (It increased from less than a fifth to two-thirds of the nondefense budget.) A similar pattern has emerged in local government budgets; expenditures for these services reached 60 percent in 1970.

SUMMARY

The starting point for determining the sensible limits to government is an examination of the goods and services needed in a modern society. Two important properties are useful for classifying goods and services: exclusion and joint consumption. A good is characterized as having the property of exclusion if its acquisition or use can readily be denied by the supplier. A suit of clothes has this property; the fish in the sea do not. A good is characterized as a joint-consumption good or an individual-consumption good depending on whether it can or cannot be consumed jointly and simultaneously by many users.

TV broadcasting is a joint-consumption good; a loaf of bread is not.

Goods can be classified according to the degree to which they possess these two properties. The result is four idealized types of goods: private goods (characterized by exclusion and individual consumption), toll goods (exclusion and joint consumption), common-pool goods (nonexclusion and individual consumption), and collective goods (nonexclusion and joint consumption).

Private goods and toll goods are supplied by the marketplace, and collective action plays a relatively minor role with respect to such goods, primarily establishing ground rules for market transactions, ensuring the safety of some private goods, and regulating those toll goods that are natural monopolies. However, collective action is indispensable for assuring a continued supply of common-pool goods and collective goods, and for providing those private and toll goods that society decides are to be subsidized and supplied as though they were collective goods.

More and more private and toll goods have been redefined, in essence, and are being treated as collective or common-pool goods. Indeed, the big growth in government has taken place in expenditures for such redefined goods. This has occurred both at federal and local levels. Such goods now comprise almost half of federal spending (two-thirds of nondefense spending) and three-fifths of local government spending. Providing goods and services that are intrinsically collective by nature, which is one of the fundamental reasons for the creation and existence of governments, is no longer the principal activity of governments in the United States. Government growth has meant growth in government supply of noncollective goods.

NOTES

1. The following typology employing these concepts draws heavily on Vincent and Elinor Ostrom, "Public Goods and Public Choices," in *Alternatives for Delivering Public Services,* ed. E.S. Savas (Boulder, Colo.: Westview Press, 1977), pp. 7-14.
2. One could conceive of the following way to transform a lighthouse into an excludable good: Instead of a conventional lighthouse, a radio beacon could be used. Only paying subscribers who were supplied with the proper receivers and provided with regular information about the frequency currently in use could avail themselves of the service. (I'd like to have the lifeboat concession in the vicinity of such a beacon.)
3. William Vickrey, "Optimization of Traffic and Facilities," *Journal of Transport Economics and Policy* 1, no. 2 (May 1967): 123-36.

CHAPTER 4

ALTERNATIVE WAYS
TO PROVIDE SERVICES

In the preceding chapter we saw the role of collective action with respect to supplying each of the four kinds of goods. For those goods that are intrinsically — that is, by their nature and prior to any redefinition — private goods or toll goods or common-pool goods, collective action is needed primarily for regulation. In effect, such regulation is a collective good created to assure satisfactory supplies of those three kinds of goods.

With respect to collective goods, collective action is necessary to pay for the goods and thereby make sure that they are produced and available. For private goods and toll goods assigned — deliberately or not — the properties of common-pool goods, collective action is needed for deciding on such redefinitions and to provide the subsidy or the payment in full that is decided on.

The essence of collective action, it is therefore clear, consists of making decisions and raising money. This is true of all the collective actions we have described, for all four kinds of goods.

Stating those functions in this way makes it readily apparent that collective action is by no means synonymous with government action. Groups of people can and do agree on collective decisions and collective fund raising even without the formal status and sanctions available to governments. For example, Little Leagues and recreation facilities such as beaches, swimming pools, golf courses, tennis courts, flower gardens, and cultural institutions are often provided as collective goods; but identical services and facilities are also provided as toll goods by voluntary membership associations (and by private, profit-making organizations, for that matter). People interested in consuming one or more of these common recreation services agree to form a club and to pay for the desired facility through membership dues, entrance fees, and other collective fund-raising actions. Carpools and vanpools represent more informal collective activity.

It might be argued that these instances of voluntary collective action are possible only because the goods are intrinsically toll goods, and exclusion is therefore possible. Can voluntary associations take collective action to provide collective goods where exclusion is truly infeasible? The answer is yes. An example can be seen in cities with enclaves of private streets. The care and maintenance of these streets is provided by home-owner, civic, or neighborhood associations. Money to pay for street cleaning, snow removal, and sometimes even private police patrol is obtained from local residents through membership dues or pro rata user charges.

Collective action in such circumstances may not be completely voluntary; it may be a requirement or covenant written into the property deed itself so that anyone buying a house in that area knows he is required to belong to the association and to pay a just portion of the expenses of the association, in exchange for voting rights in it. Housing cooperatives and condominiums have similar features.

But collective action can be entirely voluntary and still be effective in providing collective goods. When the collective organization is relatively small and the members have similar values and similar interests, informal social pressures can be adequate to assure that everyone contributes his or her fair share and no one is a free rider. A volunteer fire department is an excellent and commonplace example. Tenant patrols and block patrols in crime-ridden areas of large cities are other examples of successful voluntary collective action used to provide collective goods. (Payment can be in the form of contributed services, rather than money.) So are the associations in unincorporated communities that, despite their lack of government authority, nevertheless contract with private firms for refuse-collection service to their members. (However, like the recreation goods mentioned above and unlike fire protection and safety patrols, refuse collection is more of a toll good, and the service can be denied to any would-be free rider.)

It is when the number of affected individuals becomes large and interests are diverse and conflicting that purely voluntary action is no longer adequate to provide collective goods. In such circumstances organizations have to be created with the authority to exercise force to take the money or property that is deemed necessary to assure the supply of collective goods. In short, *government can be viewed as nothing more than an instrument for making and enforcing decisions about collective goods:* which ones to provide, which ones (of those that are intrinsically private or toll goods) are to be financed at least in part by involuntary collective contributions, how to allocate the costs or contributions, and how to allocate the goods themselves if they are not pure collective goods.

All collective goods require collective action, but we have seen that not all collective action need be taken by governments. Nevertheless, the role of government is so pervasive and so dominant with respect to collective goods that henceforth in this inquiry, where no ambiguity will be introduced, we will use the term *government* to mean collective action, collective decision, or instrument of collective will. Thus, when we say *government* provides for national defense, that is a shorthand way of expressing the notion that collective action was taken to decide that national defense is needed and to give the government all necessary means to obtain that particular good.

The reader who has managed to remain alert up to this point will have noticed the noncommittal verbs used to describe the role of government with respect to goods: provide, supply, assure the availability of, arrange payment for, and so on. Nothing that has been said so far requires that collective goods be delivered by government workers. They may be produced directly by public employees working for public agencies, but they need not be. Many other institutional arrangements also exist for delivering collective goods. For example, governments purchase services from private firms, and toll goods are sold by private organizations both under exclusive franchises and under conditions of competition.

Service Elements

Before discussing the different institutional arrangements for providing services, important distinctions must be made among the service consumer, the service producer, and the service arranger.

The consumer directly obtains or receives the service. The consumer might be an individual, a household, everyone residing in a defined geographic area, or a class of individuals with common characteristics, such as poor people, students, exporters, mental retardates, or farmers.

The service producer is the agent that actually and directly performs the work or delivers the service to the consumer. A producer can be a unit of government (local, county, state, or federal), a multipurpose or unifunctional special district, a voluntary association of citizens, a private firm, a nonprofit agency, or, in certain instances, the consumer himself. The Department of Defense produces national defense services, as does Lockheed. A county government may produce public health services. A tenant association produces a service when it patrols its building. A doctor produces services when he treats Medicaid patients. An individual who hauls his own trash to the town dump is acting as both producer and consumer of the service.

The service arranger is the agent who assigns the producer to the consumer, or vice versa, or selects the producer who will serve the consumer. Frequently, but not always, the arranger is a government unit. Thus, the service arranger may be the municipality in which the consumer is located, the federal government, a voluntary association, or the service consumer himself. For collective goods the arranger can usefully be viewed as the collective-decision unit, that is, the unit that articulates the demand for such goods.

When a city government hires a paving contractor to resurface a street with asphalt, the city is the arranger, the firm is the producer, and the public at large is the consumer of this particular collective good—the repaved street. A state government is the service arranger when it contracts with a church group, the producer, to operate a day-care center for working mothers, the consumers. A National Merit Scholarship winner is a consumer of educational services, but he is also acting as service arranger when he selects the college of his choice to produce his educational services.

With respect to collective goods, the arranger has significant responsibilities. He must have authority to levy taxes, assessments, or user charges despite a lack of unanimous consent, relying instead on rules established, for example, by majority vote, either directly or through representatives. Similarly, on the demand side, the arranger must establish procedures to decide on the services to be provided, the level of service, and the level of expenditures to be made, again in the absence of unanimous agreement among all the members of the collective unit.

At this point we are ready to list and discuss the alternative institutional arrangements or structures utilized to deliver services. The following different arrangements can be identified, and each will be examined in turn:

1. Government service
2. Intergovernmental agreement

3. Contract, or purchase of service
4. Franchise
5. Grant
6. Voucher
7. Free market
8. Voluntary service
9. Self-service

GOVERNMENT SERVICE

The term *government service* denotes the delivery of a service by a government agency using its own employees; that is, the same government unit acts as both the service arranger and the service producer. Examples of municipal, county, state, and federal government services abound, and it is not necessary to illustrate or elaborate further.

INTERGOVERNMENTAL AGREEMENT

A government can hire or pay another government to supply a service. A local school district does just that when, lacking a high school of its own, it arranges to send its pupils to the high school in a neighboring town and pays the latter jurisdiction for the service. It is also commonplace for small communities to purchase library, recreation, and fire-protection services from a specialized government unit that is organized by and sells its service to several general-purpose governments in the area. Counties sometimes contract with cities and pay the latter to maintain county roads within city limits. States contract with cities and counties to provide social services to families and individuals. Reassignment of service responsibilities between jurisdictions is occurring to a significant degree in an attempt to better handle regional problems and cope with rising costs.[1] We refer to such institutional arrangements as *inter-*

governmental agreements. One government is the producer but another is the service arranger.

Intergovernmental agreements are common. A 1973 survey of 2,375 municipalities in the United States revealed that no less than 62 percent had formal or informal agreements for the provision of services to their citizens by other government units. Moreover, 43 percent of all cities produced services for other governments.[2] The relative roles of different service producers is shown in table 4.1. Counties were the most common producers of services under intergovernmental agreements. Other municipalities serve as producers for 40 percent of the cities with intergovernmental agreements. Services commonly provided under intergovernmental agreements include water supply, sewage treatment, jails, police communications, libraries, animal control, resource recovery plants, and public health services.

TABLE 4.1

Producers of Services to Municipalities
Under Intergovernmental Agreements

Government Producer	Frequency
County	62%
Municipality	40
State	29
Special district	28
(Other than school)	
School district	25
Public authority	17

NOTE: That is, 62 percent of the municipalities that received one or more services through intergovernmental agreements identified the county as the producer. (Total adds to more than 100 percent because many cities arrange for services from more than one kind of producer.)

SOURCE: Derived from *The Challenge of Local Governmental Reorganization,* vol. 3 (U.S. Government Printing Office, Advisory Commission on Intergovernmental Relations, February 1974), table 3.3. Data are from a 1973 survey.

The Lakewood Plan makes extensive use of this particular institutional arrangement for service delivery. In 1981 the city of Lakewood, in Los Angeles County, was purchasing 41 different services from the county; 76 other cities also purchased one or more services from the county. All 77 cities purchased election services from the county, and other county services being marketed included animal regulation; emergency ambulance service; enforcement of health ordinances; engineering services; fire and police protection; library; sewer maintenance; park maintenance; recreation services; assessment and collection of taxes; hospitalization of city prisoners; personnel staff services such as recruitment, examination, and certification; prosecution; building inspection; weed abatement; school fire-safety officers; mobile-home and trailer-park inspection; milk inspection; rodent control; mental health services; tree trimming; bridge maintenance; preparation and installation of street signs; street sweeping; traffic-signal maintenance; traffic striping and marking; traffic-law enforcement; business license issuing and enforcement; and crossing guards.

CONTRACT OR PURCHASE OF SERVICES

Governments contract not only with other governments but also with private firms and nonprofit organizations for delivery of goods and services. The U.S. Mint contracts out part of its coin-production work. Defense contracts are a major expenditure item for the federal government and are used not only for equipment and for "think-tank" services but even for direct defense activities. A private contractor mans and operates the Distant Early Warning line that detects airplanes and missiles coming toward North America over the Arctic Ocean. The U.S. government purchased the services of a private firm to carry out monitoring and surveillance of the cease-fire line in Sinai between Egyptian and Israeli forces, a task that traditionally would be performed by a military unit. Mercenary troops have been used since ancient times and are still being used today in clandestine wars. Private air forces have come into being in recent years to engage in war under contract.

At the municipal level, more benign contracts with private firms are used to provide refuse collection, ambulance service, street paving, and traffic-light maintenance, and to operate centers for senior citizens, for example. In contract service, government is the service arranger and a private organization is the service producer.

Most of the tangible goods—the supplies, equipment, and facilities—used by governments in the United States are purchased from contractors; little manufacturing, construction, or food production is performed by government employees. This is true even of sensitive military supplies, for even though munitions are manufactured in some federal arsenals, most are obtained from private producers. And it is certainly true at the local level, where roads, schools, and government offices are generally constructed for governments by private builders under contractual arrangements, and pencils, desks, fire hoses, uniforms, food (for pupils, patients, and prisoners), ferry boats, automobiles, guns, garbage trucks, and computers are bought from private vendors.

Intangible services, too, are obtained to a significant degree by contract. It is estimated that the U.S. Department of Defense alone spent somewhere between $8 billion and $13 billion for contract services in fiscal 1978, thereby indirectly providing employment for about half a million civilian workers in private firms.[3] Of the activities classified as commercial and industrial in the Defense Department—functions such as food service, laundry, airplane and vehicle maintenance, and construction—about a quarter of the total effort, measured in man-years, was purchased from the private sector.[4] An estimated $42 billion was spent in 1976 by governments in the United States on purchased services, including both intergovernmental and private contracts.[5]

No comprehensive information is available on the amount of money spent by municipal governments for contract services, but table 4.2 shows the number of cities, out of a total sample of 2,375 cities, that contract with private, profit-making firms for the indicated services.

The first thing that strikes one on seeing table 4.2 is the extraordinarily lengthy and incredibly diverse list of services available by contract from private firms. No less than 66 services were identified in that survey, and yet even this list is not complete; custodial services for government buildings and grounds are also obtained through this arrangement, as are lunchroom operations in schools and government office buildings; demolition work; operation of auditoriums and convention centers; tree pruning, tree removal, planting, grass mowing, lawn and golf-course maintenance, weed abatement, and other horticultural services; traffic-signal maintenance; towing away of illegally parked and abandoned automobiles; processing parking tickets; traffic striping and marking; parking lot operations; bus shelters; school bus transportation; vehicle maintenance; street sweeping, leaf collection; maintenance of communication equipment, key punching, and data processing services; test scoring; laundry services; secretarial and clerical work; water-meter maintenance; and management consulting. Such social services as day care, foster-home care, group-home care, adoption, institutional care, rehabilitative services, family counseling, child protection, homemaker services, and legal aid for impoverished defendants are obtained by state and local government contracts with private firms and nonprofit institutions.[6] (In 1976, of the $750 million spent for social services under Title XX of the Social Security Act, at least a third went to private organizations for the purchase of such services.[7])

As noted in table 4.2, specialized police services such as crime laboratories and police communication are procured by contract, but to a limited extent; patrol services, too, have

TABLE 4.2
The Number of Cities Using Private Firms to Supply Municipal Services Under Contract

Service	Number of Cities Contracting With Private Firms
Refuse Collection	339
Street Lighting	309
Electricity Supply	258
Engineering Services	253
Legal Services	187
Ambulance Services	169
Solid Waste Disposal	143
Utility Billing	104
Animal Control	99
Planning	92
Water Supply	84
Mapping	74
Water Distribution System	67
Payroll	65
Street Construction and Maintenance	63
Hospitals	57
Special Transportation Services	49
Cemeteries	47
Microfilm Services	47
Nursing Services	34
Assessing	31
Public Relations	30
Bridge Construction and Maintenance	25
Industrial Development	24
Tax Collection	24
Mental Health	22
Sewage Disposal	21
Management Service for Publicly Owned Transit	18
Electrical and Plumbing Inspection	17
Libraries	17
Zoning and Subdivision Control	16
Sewer Lines	14

TABLE 4.2 *(continued)*

Treasury Functions	14
All Fire Services	13
Mosquito Control	12
Museums	12
General Development	10
Alcoholic Rehabilitation	9
Records Maintenance	9
Election Administration	8
Police Communications	8
Building and Mechanical Inspection	7
Fire Communications	7
Housing	7
Recreational Facilities	7
Personnel Services	6
Urban Renewal	6
Crime Laboratory	5
Irrigation	5
Parks	5
Traffic Control	5
Water Pollution Abatement	5
All Public Health Services	4
Juvenile Delinquency Program	4
Licensing	4
Soil Conversion	4
Civil Defense Communications	2
Fire Prevention	2
Noise Abatement	2
Patrol Services	2
Registration of Voters	2
Training of Firemen	2
Air Pollution Abatement	1
Jails and Detention Homes	1
Welfare	1

NOTE: Based on responses of 2,375 cities to a mail survey in 1973.

SOURCE: Derived from *The Challenge of Local Governmental Reorganization,* vol. 3 (Washington, D.C.: U.S. Government Printing Office, Advisory Commission on Intergovernmental Relations, February 1974), appendix table 3.A.

been provided in parks, public housing projects, airports, and schools through contracting, and so have investigative services to combat organized crime and narcotics distribution.[8]

Recent data on refuse collection show that 21 percent of U.S. cities contract with private firms for this service.[9] A study of twenty-six municipal services in eighty-four California cities found that city departments produced only 50 percent of these services, while contracts with private firms accounted for 20 percent, and intergovernmental contracts with counties and special districts accounted for 15 percent and 10 percent respectively.[10]

Interesting examples of contracting for services can be found abroad. Most of the cities in Denmark contract with a single private firm for fire and ambulance service; the majority of the population of the country receives protection through this arrangement. About two-thirds of the people in Sweden get their fire protection services from private enterprises under contract to government.[11] And while Wall Street is cleaned by a government bureaucracy, the streets in Communist Belgrade are cleaned by a worker-owned enterprise that has a contract with the city government.

It is worth noting at this point that, in general, broad services can be fractionated and considered in terms of their component subservices, which can be provided through various arrangements. Thus, police services can be separated into police communication, preventive patrol, traffic control, parking enforcement, towing away illegally parked cars, homicide investigation, detention facilities, training courses, and so forth.[12] The different components of this large array of services can be provided through a variety of institutional structures in the same city: government service, intergovernmental contracts, contracts with private firms, and voluntary service, for example.

One final point is that a contract can have a negative price; that is, the private producer could pay the government for the privilege of performing the service. For example, abandoned automobiles in New York City are picked up by private firms under contract to the city, and depending on scrap prices, their bids will call for payment either to or from the city. This might also be true of waste-paper collection, or of collection of any recyclable material.

FRANCHISES

Franchising is another institutional structure used for providing services. An exclusive franchise is an award of monopoly privileges to a private firm to supply a particular service, usually with price regulation by a government agency. Nonexclusive or multiple franchises can also be awarded, as in the case of taxis. In franchise service, as in contract service, government is the arranger and a private organization is the producer of the service; however, the two can be distinguished by the means of payment to the producer. Government pays the producer for contract services, but the consumer pays the producer for franchise service.

The franchise arrangement is particularly suitable for providing toll goods. Common utilities such as electric power, gas and water distribution, telephone service, and cable television are usually provided as franchise services, and so is bus transportation. Note that many of these services are provided directly by government in some jurisdictions: Local governments own and operate many electric plants, water supply systems, and bus lines, for example, and in Anchorage, Alaska, the telephone system is a municipal service. Concessions in parks, stadiums, airports, and other public properties are also franchises.

GRANTS

Toll goods and private goods whose consumption is to be encouraged can be subsidized and provided through two different structural arrangements: grants or vouchers. Under a grant system, the subsidy is given by government to the producer, typically by direct grants of money but often by grants of tax-exempt status. Examples of this arrangement are the government-induced provision of low-cost housing by the private real estate industry, and subsidized mass transit. The intended effect of such grants is to reduce the price of the particular toll good for certain eligible consumers who can then go into the marketplace and purchase for themselves from the subsidized producers more than they could afford to consume.

Under a grant arrangement the producer is a private firm (either profit-making or not), both the government and the consumer are involved as co-arrangers (the government selects certain producers to receive grants, and the consumer chooses the specific producer), and usually both government and the consumer make payments to the producer.

There are numerous examples of grants in practice. It seems as though every single industry has had some special grant or tax-abatement program tailored for it; subsidies of milk and other farm products are merely the more obvious examples of such programs. Universities have long been the beneficiaries of grants, and health facilities have also been receiving large grants over a prolonged period of time as a means of making medical care more available and accessible to more people.

Cultural institutions and performing arts groups are the latest beneficiaries of government grants, reflecting a recent collective determination that these goods benefit the public at large and therefore their availability should be encouraged by subsidies to theater groups, symphony orchestras, opera companies, dance ensembles, and museums.

VOUCHERS

The voucher system is also designed to encourage the consumption of particular goods by a particular class of consumers. Unlike the grant system that subsidizes the producer and restricts the consumer's choice to the subsidized producers only (if he wishes to avail himself of the subsidy), the voucher system subsidizes the consumer and permits the latter to exercise relatively free choice in the marketplace. Thus, rent vouchers can be contrasted with low-cost housing supplied by grants. The voucher has a certain monetary value, say $100 per month. The consumer can select the housing of his choice, and if the rent is $150 per month, he pays the landlord $50 and also gives him the voucher. The landlord takes the voucher, turns it in to the specified government agency, and receives $100 for it.

In voucher systems, as in grant systems, the producer is a private firm, and both government and the consumer pay the producer; but whereas in the grant arrangement both government and the consumer select the producer, in the voucher arrangement the consumer alone makes the choice. Nevertheless, the producer must be authorized by the government to provide the service. Not anyone can turn in rent vouchers to the government and get cash; only a legitimate property owner can do so.

Food stamps are another example of a voucher system. Instead of setting up a whole new government-run food-distribution system to give away food to eligible poor recipients, the latter are supplied with vouchers that they can use in ordinary, existing food stores. The consumer is strongly motivated to shop wisely and look for bargains because his money will then go farther and he can buy more; his behavior as a subsidized consumer should be indistinguishable from that of an unsubsidized consumer. (This can be contrasted with the situation mentioned earlier where government gives away food, virtually as a common-pool good, in school and summer lunch programs. The consumer behaves very differently in those cases and has no motivation to take only the food he will eat.)

The GI Bill of Rights after the Second World War featured a voucher system that enabled veterans to attend college by giving them, in effect, tuition money. Note the profound difference between this approach and a state university. The latter is a government institution where public funds are given to professors and administrators to dispense education services to eligible consumers. On the other hand, under the GI Bill tuition money was given to the student to spend in the college of his choice. Of course, only accredited institutions could provide education services to veterans; fly-by-night schools were not eligible purveyors of that good, and a veteran attending such a school would not receive his tuition stipend.

A Medicaid or a Medicare enrollment card is essentially a voucher for medical service. Instead of having to go to a government hospital for medical care, the cardholder can select the doctor of his choice at any facility. This is not as good a voucher system as food stamps or the GI Bill, however, because there is no incentive for the consumer to seek out a low-cost, good-quality producer; reimbursement rates are fixed, and if a person finds a doctor who charges less then the maximum, the savings will not accrue to the consumer but to the federal agency that pays the bill.

Voucher systems have also been introduced for cultural activities, as an alternative to the grant system. Instead of giving grants to theaters, cultural vouchers are given to individuals to encourage their attendance, and the voucher holder can attend the performance of his choice. The theater takes his or her voucher and is reimbursed for it.[13]

MARKET

The market system is used to provide private goods and many toll goods. The consumer himself arranges for service and selects the producer, which is a private firm. Government is not involved in the transaction in any significant way, although it may establish service standards. For example, a not uncommon arrangement in small American cities for refuse collection is mandatory private collection, where the municipal government establishes a requirement that all households have their refuse collected at least once a week, let's say, but it is left up to each household to select and pay a private firm to provide this service.

Voluntary Service

We saw above that many services that in some communities are provided as government services are available in other communities through a voluntary collective arrangement. Cited as examples were recreation facilities, street cleaning, protective patrol, and fire protection. In this arrangement, the voluntary mutual-aid association acts as service arranger and either produces the service directly, using its members as workers, or hires and pays a private firm to do the work. When a voluntary association engages in the business of supplying private goods, such as a housing or food cooperative, it is really no different from a private, nonprofit firm operating in the free market.

Although such arrangements are widespread, there is little information available as to the precise extent to which they are utilized, except for volunteer fire departments; these constitute more than 90 percent of all fire departments in the United States.[14]

Self-Service

The most basic delivery mode of all is self-help, or self-service. Protection against fire and theft is obtained primarily by rudimentary self-service measures, such as extinguishing cigarettes and locking doors. The individual who brings his newspapers to a recycling center, drives to work, bandages a cut, or gives vocational guidance to his child is practicing self-service. The family as a self-service unit is the original and most efficient department of health, education, and welfare. It provides a wide range of vital services to its members, and a minute but increasing number of families is braving formidable bureaucratic forces by teaching children at home instead of sending them to school.[15]

SERVICE COMBINATIONS

While a particular service is generally provided through one or perhaps two different arrangements in a particular culture or society, some services may be provided under several arrangements. One of the most tractable services in this respect is residential refuse collection; no less than eight of the nine arrangements can be found somewhere in the United States.

1. Municipal collection is commonplace, particularly in large cities.
2. In a number of areas special districts have been formed to provide solid-waste collection and disposal services, and a local municipality enters into an agreement with it for its services.
3. Contract collection is widespread, as noted above; the locality hires and pays a private firm to do the work.
4. Franchise collection is common on the West Coast. The city awards a territorially exclusive privilege to one private firm and regulates the latter's rates. The firm services all the households in its area and bills the households for the work.
5. In many communities, the free market is relied upon to provide this service. An individual household chooses one of several private firms engaged in this business locally and pays the firm directly.

6. Voluntary arrangements can also be found. For example, in Kansas City, Missouri, homeowner associations in various neighborhoods can make their own arrangements for refuse collection; they hire private firms to provide the customized service they desire, and pay for it by levying charges on their members.

7. Self-service is another ubiquitous form. Small towns throughout the country generally have a disposal site nearby, "the town dump," where residents can often be found on Saturday morning sociably discarding their accumulated household rubbish.

8. In St. Paul, Minnesota, a grant arrangement was utilized in part. A user fee was charged for this service by the municipal agency, but low-income residents paid only half-price; taxes were used to supplement the agency budget, thereby enabling it to provide the service at a discount to the eligible households.

As far as the author is aware, of the nine different arrangements, only the voucher system is not utilized to provide this service in the United States.

It should be pointed out that more than one arrangement can be employed by the same jurisdiction for the same service. For example, in Indianapolis five different arrangements are utilized for the collection of residential refuse: municipal service, contract service, voluntary service, free market, and self-service.[16] Not only is there nothing necessarily wrong with using multiple structures simultaneously for the same service, but by fostering comparisons and competition among the different service producers, the result may well be superior performance of that service in that city. This point is pursued further in a later chapter.

In addition to the *multiple* arrangement discussed in the preceding paragraph — the use of more than one arrangement to provide the same service in the same area — there are also *com-*

pound arrangements. This was illustrated above in the case of refuse collection in St. Paul where the municipal arrangement is combined with the grant arrangement to supply low-cost service. Similarly, a franchised bus line that receives an operating subsidy from the government also represents a compound arrangement. In other words, the nine arrangements discussed above can be thought of as pure structures, which can be combined to produce compound arrangements. The grant arrangement is the most common partner used in compound arrangements.

Summary

The nine different institutional structures or arrangements for delivering services, and the characteristic identities of producers, arrangers, and payers in each structure, are summarized in table 4.3, which makes it easy to see at a glance how the arrangements differ and how each arrangement is unique with

TABLE 4.3
Institutional Arrangements for Providing Public Services

Service Arrangement	Arranges Service	Produces Service	Pays Producer
Government service	government	government	N.A.
Intergovernmental agreement or contract	government (1)	government (2)	government (1)
Contract	government	private firm	government
Franchise	government	private firm	consumer
Grant	government and consumer	private firm	government and consumer
Voucher	consumer	private firm	government and consumer
Market	consumer	private firm	consumer
Voluntary	voluntary association	voluntary association or private firm	voluntary association
Self-service	consumer	consumer	N.A.

respect to the roles of government, consumers, firms, and voluntary associations.

NOTES

1. *Pragmatic Federalism: The Reassignment of Functional Responsibility* (Washington, D.C.: Advisory Commission on Intergovernmental Relations, July 1976).
2. *The Challenge of Local Governmental Reorganization,* vol. 3 (Washington, D.C.: Advisory Commission on Intergovernmental Relations, February 1974), tables 3.3 and 3.A.
3. Estimates by Richard U.L. Cooper, *Contract-Hire Personnel in the Department of Defense,* Publication P-5864 (Santa Monica, Calif.: RAND Corporation, April 1977).
4. *Hearings on Contracting Out of Jobs and Services, Subcommittee on Employee Ethics and Utilization, Committee on Post Office and Civil Service,* House of Representatives, Serial No. 95-7 (Washington, D.C.: U.S. Government Printing Office, 1977), p. 29.
5. Barbara J. Nelson, "Purchase of Services," in *Productivity Improvement Handbook for State and Local Governments,* ed. George Washnis (New York: Wiley, 1978).
6. For more detailed examples of contracting for local government services, see Donald Fisk, Herbert Kiesling, and Thomas Muller, *Private Provision of Public Services: An Overview* (Washington, D.C.: Urban Institute, May 1978).
7. *Title XX: Purchase of Service,* vol. 1 (Berkeley, Calif.: Pacific Consultants, October 1978).
8. See Nelson, "Purchase of Services."
9. E.S. Savas, *The Organization and Efficiency of Solid Waste Collection* (Lexington, Mass.: Lexington Books, 1977), p. 51.
10. John J. Kirlin, John C. Ries, and Sidney Sonenblum, "Alternatives to City Departments," in *Alternatives for Delivering Public Services,* ed. E.S. Savas (Boulder, Colo.: Westview Press, 1977).
11. Robert L. Bish and Robert Warren, "Scale and Monopoly Problems in Urban Government Services," *Urban Affairs Quarterly* 8 (September 1972): 97-120.

12. Elinor Ostrom, Roger B. Parks, and Gordon P. Whitaker, *Patterns of Metropolitan Policing* (Lexington, Mass.: Lexington Books, 1976).

13. Gary Bridge, "Citizen Choice in Public Service: Voucher Systems," in Savas, *Alternatives for Delivering Public Services.*

14. See Fisk, Kiesling, and Muller, "Private Provision of Public Services: An Overview."

15. "Teaching Children at Home," *Time,* 4 December 1978, p. 78.

16. See Savas, *Organization and Efficiency,* p. 34.

CHAPTER 5

ANALYSIS OF THE ALTERNATIVES

We have seen that no less than nine different institutional arrangements (or structures or mechanisms) exist for providing services to the public: government service, intergovernmental agreement, contract or purchase of service, franchise, grant, voucher, market, voluntary, and self-service. These seem to offer ample opportunity to limit government growth while assuring satisfactory provision of services. Can each arrangement be used for any service? If not, in what circumstances or for what kinds of services can each be used? What are the relative advantages and disadvantages of each? If more than one arrangement can be used to deliver a particular service, which is best? In what way?

THE NATURE OF THE GOODS AND THE CHOICE OF ARRANGEMENTS

One can start answering these questions by referring to the intrinsic nature of the service in question. Private goods can be provided by grant, voucher, or market arrangements or by self-service. In the United States, such goods are not supplied by government, intergovernmental agreement, contract, or franchise arrangements, although in principle they could be and in some countries they are. For example, in the Soviet Union most retail shops are operated as a municipal service.

Toll goods, which are like private goods in that they are subject to exclusion, can be provided through any of the nine arrangements.

Collective goods can be supplied by government, by intergovernmental agreement, by contract, or by a voluntary arrangement. They cannot be provided through franchises, grants, vouchers, or the marketplace, as these structures all require exclusion to be effective, and collective goods, by definition, do not possess this property. (The reader may recall the lighthouse in chapter 3 as an example of a collective good whose use cannot effectively be denied to any would-be user.)

Goods that are intrinsically common-pool goods are provided by nature, but we have seen that government action can, in effect, create such goods and give them away, in which case government service, intergovernmental agreements, contracts, grants, or vouchers can be used to supply them; free lunch programs and medical care have been identified previously as falling into this class of government-created common-pool goods. (It should be recognized that voluntary arrangements can create and supply such goods, as exemplified by a charitable organization that offers food and shelter to the needy.)

TABLE 5.1

*Types of Goods and Institutional Arrangements
That Can Be Used for Their Delivery*

Arrangement	Private Goods	Toll Goods	Collective Goods	Common- Pool Goods
Government service		X	X	X
Intergovernmental agreement		X	X	X
Contract		X	X	X
Franchise		X		
Grant	X	X		X
Voucher	X	X		X
Market	X	X		
Voluntary		X	X	X
Self-service	X			

The situation is summarized in table 5.1 on page 77, which shows the different arrangements that can be used to supply each of the different kinds of goods. The table makes it clear that each kind can be provided through more than one institutional arrangement. The next step is to see what further attributes or characteristics of the goods and the arrangements are important in determining the suitability of a particular arrangement for supplying a particular good.

CHARACTERISTICS OF SERVICES

Specificity

Some services can be specified precisely with little ambiguity and little chance of misunderstanding. Other services cannot be specified so precisely and allow much room for reasonable people to differ significantly in their interpretations of what the service entails. Compare, for example, street paving and education. The former can be described in precise engineering terms with detailed technical specifications as to the depth and type of foundation, the thickness and quality of asphalt overlay, provisions for drainage, and so forth. Education cannot be specified in any terms remotely comparable, and so the requests to "pave this street" and "educate this child" will produce very different responses among potential service providers. Producers of paving services can proceed to estimate the cost of the work and can submit bids to do it. The service arranger can readily compare bids, and in due course, he can inspect the work while in progress and on completion. He can then state, with relatively little margin for error, that the requested service was or was not performed. On the other hand, producers of educational services, faced with the hypothetical request for proposals to "educate this child," may plausibly design a widely differing range of educational programs even if the service arranger, prevailed upon to be more specific, goes on to define education as involving reading, writing, and arithmetic. It is not even sufficient to say that the child will be considered educated if he or she can pass a certain examination. The range of information and the kinds of skills that the child should have acquired and will have to demonstrate can ultimately be defined only by reference to a specific curriculum and study materials. If the service arranger goes this far in describing the desired service to potential producers, he is then, in effect, doing nothing more than hiring a teacher.

The fact that some services can be specified to a much greater degree than others means that some arrangements that are feasible for the former are less feasible or infeasible for the latter. Specifiable services permit preparation of intelligible requests for service, submission of proposals that conform with the request, and evaluation of performance. Services that cannot be specified in detail cannot elicit this series of actions. Services run the full gamut from those that can be specified in great detail to those that can be defined only in rather broad and general terms. The former can readily be provided by any of the arrangements; the latter kind of service cannot, in general. In particular, poorly defined services cannot easily be provided by intergovernmental agreement, by contract, by franchise, or by grant. (An exception occurs if a service is already being performed, in which case a service arranger says, in effect, "I like what you're doing and I'd like to buy some of it, too." This is what happens when a school district sends its students to a school in a neighboring district, for instance.)

If a service cannot be specified very well, how can anyone or any arrangement supply it satisfactorily? In particular, how can a government agency or anyone else perform a service satisfactorily if it is not at all clear what the service calls for, and what "satisfactory" means? Only with difficulty is the answer. That is, only with close supervision, extensive monitoring, frequent feedback from the consumer to the producer, close coordination between upper and lower echelons of the produc-

ing organization, frequent adjustments and corrections, and—
in effect—constant negotiation between the consumer and the
producer to balance expectations, capabilities, and achievements. These conditions can best be achieved where no third
party stands between the consumer and producer, a situation
realized when the consumer is the arranger (e.g., Medicare)
and also when the arranger is the producer (e.g., police protection). Table 4.3 in the preceding chapter shows that the former
circumstance obtains under market and voucher arrangements, and the latter under government, voluntary, and—of
course—self-service arrangements.

Availability of Producers

For some services, many producers are already in existence or
can readily be encouraged to enter the field; in other cases,
there are few producers and it is difficult to attract more, either
because a large capital investment may be needed or for other
reasons. This factor, too, affects the choice of service arrangement, as contract, market, and voucher arrangements will
work satisfactorily only if there are relatively many producers
from whom to choose.

CHARACTERISTICS OF
INSTITUTIONAL ARRANGEMENTS

All other things being equal, which is the arrangement of
choice for any given service? To answer this requires evaluating the arrangements according to the three fundamental criteria of service performance: efficiency, effectiveness, and
equity.

Competition

One of the most fundamental determinants of the efficiency of
any arrangement is competition; that is, the degree of competition that an arrangement permits will, to a significant degree,

determine how efficiently that arrangement will supply a service. Provided that there are enough producers to select from, market, contract, and voucher systems are most conducive to fostering competition and thereby achieving economic efficiency.

Franchising, grants, intergovernmental contracting, and voluntary arrangements permit some degree of competition, although not as great as the aforementioned three. Government service, on the other hand, generally operates as an unrivaled monopoly, despite the fact that relatively few such services are natural monopolies. Government bureaus that provide monopoly services behave like unregulated monopolies and are institutionally subject to all the inefficiencies and inadequacies inherent in such a situation. (Of course, government monopolies do not maximize profits per se, but they can otherwise take advantage of their position to maximize their budgets or the total remuneration — monetary and nonmonetary — of their employees per unit of work).

For the sake of completeness, it should be noted that self-service is like government service in that neither admits of competition. Both arrangements can be characterized as having a single, monopoly producer — but the effects will be very different in this case as the producer and the consumer are one and the same.

Consumer Choice

The principle of consumer choice has a revered position in democratic societies. Over the long run, efficient and effective service is most likely to be institutionalized when the consumer can choose among several producers. Only the market and voucher systems, and arrangements that involve multiple grants or franchises, permit any significant degree of consumer choice.

Scale

The scale of a service will generally affect its efficiency and effectiveness. The optimal scale of different services will differ, depending entirely on the technical characteristics of the production process. A one-room schoolhouse with a single teacher handling twelve different grades will not be as effective in providing a desired standard of education as a larger school with more specialized teachers, a library, laboratory, audio-visual equipment, and the like. Similarly, it is extremely inefficient for a small town with a one-man police force to have a full-time police dispatcher, a spare police car to use when the other is undergoing repair, and a full-time mechanic. At the other end of the scale, a very large police department may require so many coordinators, so many layers of supervisors, and so many reports and file clerks that it, too, is very inefficient. Some intermediate-size department is likely to be most efficient.

Government service is likely to be inefficient because the production unit must, by definition, be the same size as the consumer unit, without regard to the optimal size. Therefore, if the most efficient size for a school system is one that services 50,000 people, then cities with populations of 1,000, 10,000, 100,000, or 1 million would all be inefficient if they each had their own school system.

All the arrangements except government service (and self-service) can achieve economies of scale by allowing the size of the producer to be independent of the size of the arranger, thereby permitting the producer to be the optimal size. Inter-governmental agreements are not as inflexible as government service in this regard, but neither are they as flexible as contract or voucher arrangements, for one is limited to the size of either an existing jurisdiction or a new jurisdiction that could be created by aggregating existing ones. Contracting and franchising are quite flexible in their ability to take advantage of scale economies. If the most efficient size of a producer is smaller than the size of the jurisdiction that arranges for the service, then all well and good, for the jurisdiction could divide its territory into two or more separate areas—each of optimal size, ideally. If the jurisdiction is too small, then the franchisee or contractor can nevertheless achieve optimal size by selling its services to other nearby jurisdictions as well. (This is a feasible option even in the case of a franchise service that requires a large capital investment in a geographically circumscribed area, such as water supply or sewage treatment.)

Relating Benefits and Costs

Efficiency is more likely to be realized when there is a direct link between paying for the service and realizing its benefits, and the consumer has an economic incentive to shop wisely. Such a link exists only for private and toll goods. Within these classifications, those structures that allow a direct relationship between the paying consumer and the service producer—that is, where the consumer pays the producer directly—are market, voucher, grant, and franchise arrangements, as these do not involve any third party as an intermediary. For example, the consumer pays the grocer directly with food stamps (a voucher), and the telephone subscriber pays Ma Bell (a franchise). Voluntary service also may have this characteristic in some cases.

Government service does not interpose an intermediary between the consumer and the producer either. Unless a user charge is levied instead of a tax, however, the link between the act of paying and the act of consuming a government service is more attenuated than it is for market, voucher, grant, or franchise arrangements.

Responsiveness

Direct contact between consumer and producer would be expected to result in more responsive service as well, unless the producer has a monopoly. This relation exists when the consumer is the arranger, as in market, voucher, and grant systems, the voluntary arrangement when no contract is involved,

and the franchise arrangement when there are multiple fran-
chisees. (Of course, this is also true under self-service.)

Susceptibility to Fraud

At first glance, it appears that several of the arrangements are
particularly vulnerable to fraud, bribery, and extortion, criminal acts that, in addition to their moral impact on society, increase the cost of service. The award of government contracts,
franchises, and grants is obviously susceptible to bribery, kick-
backs, and extortion. Vouchers are vulnerable to a variety of
fraudulent schemes, as evidenced by the widespread counter-
feiting, theft, sale, and illegal redemption of food stamps.

Ideological opponents of the aforementioned arrangements
cite these weaknesses and point to the superiority of government services (and by implication, intergovernmental agreements) in this respect. Careful reflection blurs this contrast,
however. Public-sector employee unions give endorsements,
make campaign contributions, and supply campaign workers
to favored candidates for office, and are quite explicit about
their expectations when their candidate is elected; they expect
— and frequently obtain — a quid pro quo in the form of greater expenditures for the service their union produces, pay raises, and collective bargaining rules that will lead to more favor-
able outcomes of labor negotiations. They seek more jobs and
agency shops, the net effect being to enlarge the union treasury
and thereby increase the salaries and perquisites of the union
leaders.[1] While technically such behavior may be legal, in essence it differs little from the bribe paid by a private firm to secure a contract. Only voluntary and self-service arrangements
can claim immunity to such venalities.

Equity

Do the arrangements differ in their ability to provide services
to consumers in a fair and equitable manner? Some people
consider the market mechanism to be inherently inequitable in

providing public services because incomes are distributed unequally. Voluntary and franchise arrangements are subject to the same criticism insofar as the ability to obtain service is dependent on income, as in joining a country club for recreational opportunities or paying for water, electric power, or transportation. However, the other organized arrangements (that is, excluding self-service) are alike with respect to the equity issue. Grants, contracts, intergovernmental contracts, and government service can all be used to dispense services in whatever manner is deemed equitable by the appropriate government body, as can vouchers, which are deliberately designed to equalize access to services. The arrangements clearly differ in the extent to which they facilitate redistribution of goods and services in the name of equity.

Furtherance of Other Purposes

Public services can be used as a vehicle to advance other social purposes, such as regional economic development. The location of military bases in economically depressed areas of the country exemplifies this approach.

They can also be used to advance narrower political aims, such as rewarding supporters with patronage appointments. Government service is more malleable than the other arrangements for this purpose and may therefore be considered superior by elected officials, even though they have been known to use their persuasive skills on contract and franchise holders to induce them to employ the officials' deserving friends. In other words, for better or worse, government service is only slightly more convenient for advancing such ancillary purposes.

For more open goals—such as assuring equal-opportunity employment and providing jobs for the unemployed—contracts, grants, and franchises seem to serve almost as well as government service, and so do market and voucher arrangements with appropriate monitoring. After all, private firms no less than governments are subject to laws prohibiting discrimi-

nation in hiring, and private firms can be made to conform to
the letter and spirit of the law as closely as state and local governments can.

In fact, a private firm can actually be *more* responsive to
such policy direction than a government agency. Wilson and
Rachal[2] argue that it is generally easier for a public agency to
influence the behavior of a private organization than of another public agency. A number of examples can be cited to support their thesis. City housing inspectors are often better able
to persuade private landlords than public housing authorities
to correct deficiencies. In fact, a judge placed the Boston Housing Authority in receivership and castigated it, saying, "If the
BHA were a private landlord, it surely would have been driven
out of business long ago or its board jailed or most likely
both."[3] The TVA has been notably recalcitrant in reducing its
air pollution emissions despite pressure from environmental
control agencies. Local governments appear to be more successful than private firms in avoiding compliance with state environmental regulations concerning their unsanitary garbage
dumps. Perhaps the ultimate example of government agency
immunity to the law is provided by two frustrated congressmen. Exasperated by evidence that the Postal Service practiced
deceptive advertising with respect to its airmail and special delivery services, and calling it fraud, they asked for an investigation. The Federal Trade Commission declined on the grounds
that it cannot investigate another government agency.[4]

Size of Government

The size of government, measured by budget and by number
of employees, is greatest under government service and least
under market, franchise, voluntary, and self-service, of
course. Contracts, grants, and vouchers require government
expenditures but relatively few government employees because the latter are needed only to administer the programs
and not to produce the services. To the extent that these last

three arrangements are more efficient than government service, they tend to limit government spending as well; more about this in the next chapter.

Summary

The key conclusions drawn from the discussion are summarized in table 5.2 on page 88. A plus sign (or a blank) appears where the arrangement possesses (or lacks) the indicated characteristic. If the characteristic is present to some degree, or to a minor extent, this fact is denoted by the word "somewhat" or "little."

The arrangements differ substantially with respect to this array of important attributes, and no arrangement is ideal. Each has many positive features ànd lacks others. Many arrangements share each desirable feature. The conclusion to be drawn is that there is generally more than one good way to provide a service; it behooves one to recognize this when planning services and to select a delivery mode on the basis of reason rather than reflex.

NOTES

1. E. J. Dionne, Jr., "Unions Awaiting Carey's Quid Pro Quo," *New York Times,* 4 December 1978, p. B6.
2. James Q. Wilson and Patricia Rachal, "Can the Government Regulate Itself?" *Public Interest,* no. 46 (Winter 1977): 3-14.
3. Michael Knight, "Boston Housing Authority Placed in Receivership," *New York Times,* 26 July 1979, p. A12.
4. Ronald Kessler, "The Great Mail Bungle," *Washington Post,* 9 June 1974.

TABLE 5.2
Characteristics of Different Institutional Arrangements

	Government Service	Intergovernmental Agreement	Contract	Franchise	Grant	Voucher	Market	Voluntary	Self-Service
Handles poorly specified service	+					+	+	+	+
Requires multiple producers		+	+			+	+		
Encourages competition	somewhat	somewhat	+	somewhat	somewhat	+	+	somewhat	
Permits consumer choice				somewhat	somewhat	+	+	+	+
Achieves economies of scale	somewhat	somewhat	+	+	+	+	+	+	
Relates costs to benefits			+	+	+	+	+	+	+
Is responsive to consumer					+	+	+	+	+
Is invulnerable to fraud		+						+	+
Facilitates redistribution	+	+	+	+	+	+			
Furthers other purposes	somewhat	somewhat	somewhat	somewhat	somewhat	little	little	+	
Limits size of government			somewhat	+	somewhat	somewhat	+	+	+

CHAPTER 6

"PUBLIC VERSUS PRIVATE"

The previous chapters have demonstrated that there are many service arrangements and that each one has advantages and shortcomings in terms of limiting the size and growth of government. The most promising ones in this respect, those that restrict the size of government and foster efficiency through competition and by achieving scale economies, are primarily the ones that can be called private-sector alternatives: market, contract, franchise, voucher, and grant arrangements. In each of these the private sector is the producer, in contrast to governmental and intergovernmental arrangements, in which government is the producer.

Much debate, with a great deal of heat but relatively little light, has been generated on the issue of which is best, public or private production of service. With rare exceptions,[1] the battle has been waged primarily on ideological grounds by partisans of each approach. For example, advocates of "contracting out" cite the following arguments in favor of their approach compared with government production of service:

1. Contracting is more efficient because
   a. It harnesses competitive forces and brings the pressure of the marketplace to bear on inefficient producers.
   b. It permits better management, free of most of the distractions characteristic of overtly political organizations.
   c. The costs and benefits of managerial decisions are felt more directly by the decision maker, whose own rewards are directly at stake.

2. Contracting makes it possible for government to take advantage of specialized skills lacking in its own work force; it overcomes obsolete salary limitations and antiquated civil service restrictions.
3. Contracting allows flexibility in adjusting the size of a program up or down in response to changing demand and to changing availability of funds.
4. Contracting permits a quicker response to new needs and facilitates experimentation in new programs.
5. Contracting is a way of avoiding large capital outlays; it spreads costs over time at a relatively constant and predictable level.
6. Contracting permits economies of scale regardless of the scale of the government entity involved.
7. Contracting a portion of the work offers a yardstick for comparison; the cost of the service is highly visible in the price of the contract, unlike most government services.
8. Contracting can reduce dependence on a single supplier (a government monopoly) and so lessens the vulnerability of the service to strikes, slowdowns, and inept leadership.
9. Contracting limits the size of government, at least in terms of the number of employees.

The advocates of government service, often the representatives of government employee unions, offer the following rejoinders in rebuttal:

1. Contracting is ultimately more expensive because of
   a. Corruption.[2]
   b. High profits.
   c. The cost of layoffs and unemployment for government workers.
   d. The shortage of qualified suppliers and therefore the lack of competition.
   e. The cost of managing the contract and monitoring contractor performance.

    f. The low marginal cost of expanding government service.

    g. Cost-plus-fixed-fee provisions in some contracts, which provide no incentive for efficiency.

    h. The absence of effective competition in "follow-on" contracts, which are commonplace.

2. Contracting nullifies the basic principle of merit employment and subverts laws regarding veterans' preference in government employment; it is demoralizing to employees, deprives government of the skills it needs in-house, and therefore is fundamentally debilitating of government capability.

3. Contracting limits the flexibility of government in responding to emergencies.

4. Contracting fosters an undesirable dependence on contractors and leaves the public vulnerable to strikes and slowdowns by contractor personnel and to bankruptcy of the firm.

5. Contracting depends on adequately written contracts, which are difficult to draw up and as a result there is a loss of government accountability and control.

6. Contracting limits the opportunity to realize economies of scale.

7. Entrusting some services to private organizations might increase their political power to such an extent that there would be a general loss of independence for other private and public entities.

8. Contracting causes a loss of autonomy of the contractor (e.g., coopting a private, nonprofit social service agency) and therefore decreases the latter's effectiveness in the long run by muting its role as critic and social conscience.

It is obvious that these claims and counterclaims are to an extent mutually inconsistent and conflicting. The contractor is said to lose his autonomy to government and yet is held to be not accountable to nor under sufficient control of the government. It is claimed both that contracting reaps and that it dissipates economies of scale. It surmounts civil service obstacles and subverts the merit system. It increases and reduces government flexibility. It makes scarce talents available to the government and deprives government of those same talents. It is efficient and inefficient.

Some of the arguments against contracting can be turned around. For example, the argument concerning corruption was discussed in the previous chapter, and the conclusion was that the problem was symmetrical, affecting both contracting and government service in the same underlying way. As for vulnerability to service disruption, strikes by government employees have the same effect as strikes by private employees. Those who fear a loss of accountability and control under contract service seem unaware of the difficulty of holding anyone accountable in government and of the complaint often voiced by elected officials that they cannot adequately control government agencies.

The issue of which arrangement is best should properly be addressed as an empirical question, not an ideological or emotional one. There is ample room, of course, for values to enter the debate, but surely some light can be shed simply by looking at the available evidence. That is the purpose of the remainder of this chapter. The relevant criteria to use in comparing arrangements are efficiency, effectiveness, and equity. Efficiency refers to the economically efficient allocation of resources. The most efficient arrangement is the one that produces the greatest output per unit of input, for example, the lowest cost for a given level and quality of service. The most effective one is the one whose output most nearly satisfies the need; for example, meeting demands and achieving customer satisfaction as revealed by low complaint levels. An equitable arrangement permits fair distribution of the service.

We have already seen that certain arrangements cannot be utilized for certain services. Looking at services that can be provided by more than one arrangement, one expects that the services will differ as to which arrangement is best because the services themselves differ in the extent to which they possess each of the different basic attributes discussed earlier; it is not obvious that any generalization will be valid for all services.

Let us proceed to examine the available evidence, service by service. Two summaries have been attempted previously,[3] but the picture is changing rapidly.

SOLID-WASTE COLLECTION

The one service studied most extensively to determine the relative performance of different arrangements is residential solid-waste (or refuse) collection. The evidence is overwhelming and clear: Contract collection is more efficient than municipal collection. This has been determined by detailed, nationwide studies covering the United States, Canada, and Switzerland, as well as regional studies in Connecticut and the midwestern United States.[4] Municipal collection is 29 to 37 percent more costly than contract collection, while no more effective or equitable. The reasons are attributed to (1) the use of more men to do the same amount of work, (2) more absences by workers, and (3) the use of less productive vehicles.

The disparity between the two organizational forms would be even greater if one were to take into account the fact that the comparison was made between the *cost* of municipal collection and the *price* of contract collection. As this latter includes both profits and taxes, if the contract price were adjusted by excluding these factors in order to put the comparison on an equal footing, the data would show the cost of municipal service to be 61 to 71 percent greater than the cost (not price) of contract collection.

A further finding of the most definitive of the studies[5] helps explain why more cities do not utilize contract service: They do not know the true cost of their municipal service and therefore cannot compare it with an alternative. Conventional city budgets, which are not designed as cost accounting documents, generally do not reveal the full cost of collection under the category. As a result, budgets understate the true cost of this service by an average of 23 percent; that is, municipal collection costs an average of 30 percent more than the cost stated in the budget.[6]

These findings were reported in the mid-1970s and have influenced cities in their choice of arrangements. A growing number of cities are changing from municipal to contract collection.[7]

ELECTRIC POWER

Several different studies have been carried out that compare the costs of public and private electric power. For the most part, private power is supplied under regulated franchise arrangements, and so the studies compare government and franchise service.

Unfortunately, some of the studies are flawed, and no single study has effectively addressed the issue comprehensively. One study found that publicly owned utilities have significantly lower costs than privately owned utilities, but the study failed to exclude federal hydroelectric plants from the analysis, with the result that public power plants that included hydroelectric plants were compared with private plants that burned fuel.[8] Therefore the difference in findings cannot be attributed entirely to public or private ownership. This study has also been criticized on other methodological grounds.[9] Another study compared large private utilities with small municipal utilities and found the former to be more efficient; the authors conclude that private firms are better able than local governments to realize economies of scale.[10] This is clearly an important point, but the study does not provide an unambiguous comparison of public and private power. Three other investigations excluded hydroelectric generation and also controlled for the effect of size. Their findings indicate that municipal utilities are more efficient than private ones;[11] however, another study attributes the difference to tax exemptions enjoyed by municipalities.[12] To further complicate the matter, Spann concluded that private firms might be more efficient but in any event were no less efficient than municipal utilities, but his study was limited to only a few plants.[13]

In his important study, Hellman[14] found thirty-eight cities in the United States where electric power is provided by competing service producers. In effect, he compared market service with government service and government-regulated franchises and found that free market arrangements seem to lead to lower prices by private firms than does regulation, although municipal power is still lower. He argues persuasively that competition is better than regulation as a guarantee of inexpensive electricity.

DeAlessi summarizes numerous studies in the following way: Compared to private utilities, municipal utilities charge lower prices, spend more on construction, have higher operating costs, show less correlation between costs and marginal revenue, change prices less often, but do not adopt cost-reducing innovations as readily, favor business over residential users, maintain managers in officer longer, offer fewer services, and exhibit greater variation in rates of return.[15]

All in all, therefore, the picture is confused with respect to the relative virtues of public and private power supply; the definitive research has yet to be done.

FIRE PROTECTION

A private company that supplies fire protection to the city of

Scottsdale, Arizona, was carefully studied by Ahlbrandt and its cost was compared to that of traditional fire services. Ahlbrandt analyzed the cost of service in forty-nine cities serviced by paid, volunteer, and mixed fire departments (with some paid and some volunteer firemen). Because of the large sample of cities, he was able to isolate the various determinants of cost and to project what the costs would be in Scottsdale if it had one of the other service arrangements. He concluded that the cost of contract fire protection by a private firm in Scottsdale was only 53 percent of the estimated cost of supplying the service by a government agency; that is, the latter would be 89 percent more costly.[16] Thus, in the case of fire protection, contract service seems to be more efficient.

In addition to the economic comparison, observers of the firm in Arizona comment admiringly on the highly innovative and imaginative developments introduced there, including robot firefighting equipment, high-visibility paint on fire trucks, high-capacity hose, and creative staffing patterns.[17]

The successful performance of a private firefighting firm in Arizona has led to the formation of similar firms in Tennessee,[18] Georgia,[19] and elsewhere.[20] Although this is still relatively rare in the United States, in Denmark it is a long-standing practice with one firm serving about two-thirds of the population and about 85 percent of the land area.[21]

TRANSPORTATION

Airlines

An interesting comparison has been made between a public and a private trunk airline in Australia. The former is operated by a government agency, whereas the latter operates as a franchise service. Suffice it to say that both airlines are required to fly similar routes, service similar cities, use similar aircraft, and charge equal prices.

Three measures of efficiency were used to compare the airlines: tons of freight and mail carried per employee, passengers carried per employee, and earned revenue per employee. By each measure the private airline displayed greater efficiency, with ten-year means of 204 percent, 122 percent, and 113 percent respectively of the corresponding measures for the public airline.[22]

Buses

Bus services in the Federal Republic of Germany are operated both by private firms under state contracts and by the state directly. Blankart summarizes the findings and reports that the nationwide average of municipal bus transport costs are 160 percent more per kilometer than the contract price paid to private bus firms for comparable services.[23]

A much more limited study of bus operations in New York City was conducted by the State Comptroller. This was not a scientific analysis but an audit, and so it reports on an isolated local situation, and there is no reason to extrapolate the findings more broadly. Nevertheless, the results are instructive. The government bus-operating agency spent 1,518 maintenance hours per bus per year, compared with 1,025 for franchise bus operations.[24] However, no evidence is presented on miles or hours of bus operation or on the number of passengers carried per bus, which could account for differing maintenance needs.

Another study of limited scope was conducted of school buses in New York State. The report found contract bus costs to be lower than the costs of buses operated directly by school boards.[25]

POSTAL SERVICE

While no major study has compared government postal service to other alternatives because of the difficulty of finding a comparable private firm, evidence does exist in one particular area: delivering small packages. In this activity the parcel post service of the U.S. Postal Service has a very strong competitor, namely, the United Parcel Service (UPS), a private, profit-making, worker-owned enterprise.

Evidence as to their relative performance is indirect, but the following reports are suggestive: (1) UPS handles twice as many parcels as the Postal Service; (2) UPS is faster—a parcel mailed by parcel post from Washington to Los Angeles takes more than eight days, or longer than a Pony Express trip from Missouri to California in 1861; (3) UPS rates are generally cheaper; (4) the damage rate at UPS is one-fifth that of the Postal Service; (5) UPS insures every parcel up to $100 without an extra charge; (6) UPS keeps a record of each parcel; (7) UPS will pick up parcels from the mailer, for a fee; (8) UPS makes three delivery attempts, compared with one by the Postal Service; (9) in 1972 UPS earned an after-tax profit of $77 million, whereas the Postal Service lost $300 million on its tax-free parcel post business.[26]

The monopoly of the Postal Service is being attacked both theoretically and practically. The postal monopoly statutes have been questioned as being contrary to the public interest,[27] while private postal services have proliferated.[28] The ultimate indignity was suffered by the Postal Service when the General Services Administration urged all federal agencies to reduce their mail costs by using commercial carriers.[29]

HEALTH CARE

Despite the large expenditures for health care in the United States, and the concern about rising costs, there has been relatively little analysis of the effect of service organization on the cost of health care. Only a few studies of nursing homes and some limited examinations of general hospitals have been conducted.

Nursing Homes

A statistical report compared proprietary (private for-profit) with voluntary (nonprofit) and government nursing homes. It shows that the proprietary homes have lower costs per patient day and pass on the savings in the form of lower charges; they seem to achieve this result by maintaining a higher bed occupancy rate and managing with fewer employees per bed, yet the fraction of residents discharged alive (an admittedly crude measure of quality or effectiveness) is the same as other nursing homes.[30] (However, one cannot rule out the possibility that the patients in the government-run homes were sicker when admitted.)

In a study of nursing homes operated by the Veterans Administration, the average cost per patient day was found to be 83 percent higher than the cost of comparable care for similar patients placed by the VA in privately operated community nursing homes.[31] Furthermore, this comparison was biased against the private facilities because the cost of real estate, buildings, and equipment was not included in the figures for the VA-operated nursing homes, whereas it was included in the contract price charged by the private institutions.

A study in Minnesota examined 118 nursing homes to see if quality differences could be found between the different arrangements.[32] Differences were found in only 4 of 96 quality variables: Private profit-making nursing homes had more patients per room but a greater variety of physician specialties and more therapeutic services than government and voluntary (private nonprofit) nursing homes, even though they had fewer registered nurses per licensed practical nurse than the voluntary institutions.

Some evidence as to the perceived effectiveness of different kinds of nursing homes was obtained through an opinion survey of potential patients; there was no systematically higher rating for either nonprofit or for-profit nursing homes.

General Hospitals

Numerous reports speak of the benefits of private, profit-making hospitals[33] and also of contracts with private firms to manage government hospitals.[34] The tangible evidence presented to support the case is slim, however, despite the logical appeal of the position.

No cost difference was found in a study of public and private nonprofit hospitals in New York City,[35] nor was there much difference found in a study of matched pairs of for-profit and nonprofit voluntary or public hospitals.[36]

A study of perinatal mortality in New York City showed little difference between nonprofit and for-profit hospitals in one measure of effectiveness, the rate of preventable deaths. Also, the two kinds of hospitals participated equally in local government health insurance programs, which seemed to indicate equal willingness to serve high-risk, expensive patients who might not be able to pay. However, the study goes on to present data that tend to indicate lower costs for profit-making hospitals than for nonprofits. Spann cautions that the data on cost and quality were obtained separately and cannot be linked together, but concludes that the substitution of private for public health care will not lower the quality of the care, although it may lower costs.[37]

A comparison of Veterans Administration hospitals with for-profit hospitals[38] found that the latter had substantially higher per diem costs than the former, but on the other hand the average length of stay for patients in VA hospitals was substantially greater than that for patients undergoing the same surgical procedures in private hospitals. These differences were in opposite directions so that the cost per patient admitted tended toward equality in the two kinds of hospitals. With respect to the quality of hospital care, the staff/patient ratio can be used as an indicator, albeit an inadequate one; it was noted that the VA has a standard of 2:1 for general hospitals but reported an actual ratio of only 1.5:1 in 1970 while private nonprofit (voluntary) hospitals had a ratio of 2.9:1. That is, the public hospitals had a lower rating in terms of this measure of quality.

An isolated fragment that can be added to this picture is the report of New York City's comptroller that municipal hospitals had a higher rate of malpractice claims than the average hospital,[39] suggesting a lower quality of medical care in the former.

In summary, with respect to both nursing homes and general hospitals, there have been no completely satisfactory scientific studies comparing public and private institutions in a rigorous manner, but the meager evidence available suggests that nonprofit voluntary and for-profit proprietary institutions are no more costly and no lower in quality than public facilities, and may even be better in either or both respects.

Health Insurance Administration

The relative efficiency of public and private administration of health insurance has also been examined. It was found that after adjustment to assure comparability of functions, the processing cost per claim was 35 percent and 18 percent greater for public than for private administration in 1971 and 1972 respectively.[40] Four plausible reasons are offered to explain the difference: (1) competition in the private sector, which provides pressure for greater efficiency; (2) higher compensation in the public sector, ranging from 16 to 47 percent higher than corresponding jobs in the private sector; (3) incentives for private managers to maximize efficiency in the private sector, in contrast with budget-maximizing and seniority-rewarding practices among public managers; (4) greater administrative complexity in the public sector because the work of the public administrators includes not only claims processing but also extra administrative work associated with government efforts to control medical costs.

A study of for-profit and nonprofit insurance companies that were contracted by the Social Security Administration to process Medicare and Medicaid claims revealed that the for-profit firms did the work faster and had a lower error rate.[41]

Family Planning

Population control programs in Bangladesh[42] and Sri Lanka[43] by a private, voluntary agency using social marketing techniques in the marketplace appear to be twice and five times as effective, respectively, as prior efforts by local government agencies in these countries. Such programs are reported to be the most cost effective and quickly accomplished means of distributing family planning information in developing countries and to have achieved significant increase in contraceptive usage.

EDUCATION

Considering the large public expenditure for education, and the prevalence of both public and private schools, one would think that extensive research would have been conducted to compare public and private education. Unfortunately, that is not the case. Only isolated reports can be found that shed any light at all on this area.

The City of New York educates handicapped children both directly, in public schools, and also by contract, in private schools. The City Comptroller compared the two approaches and found that the per pupil cost in public schools was greater than in private schools. The public and private costs were $4,785 and $4,512 respectively for the non-severely handi-capped, and $6,196 and $4,730 for the severely handicapped.[44]

The popular appeal of private schools cannot be dismissed by claiming that they cater to quiet bigots who don't want their children to associate with children from minority groups. Minorities also prefer them,[45] at least where subsidies are available so that tuition cost is not a barrier to enrollment. In California, private Catholic schools actually have a higher proportion (40 percent) of minority pupils (mostly Hispanic) than do public schools.[46]

Comparative evidence at the university level is also sketchy. A study by the New York State Department of Education found that disadvantaged students in educational opportunity programs at private universities are graduated at much lower cost than students in similar programs at the city and state universities, although public funds are used for both. The cost to produce one such graduate from the City University was $103,061, compared with $18,570 for a private institution. The difference was attributed to more thorough screening, testing, placement, and preparation at the private universities.[47]

Harriss reviewed educational costs in public and private universities in New York City and concluded that tuition charges in private universities are considerably lower than the cost per student in the City University. He suggests a city policy of using the private universities to a much greater extent to provide higher education.[48]

Finally, an economic analysis of public and private colleges and universities[49] led to the conclusion that the public institutions operate with significantly greater labor to capital ratios; that is, they are overstaffed, comparatively speaking. The data may not be very reliable, however.

SOCIAL SERVICES

Some of the growing number of social services in the United States are being provided through contracts — by state agencies contracting with other state and with local government agencies, and by contracts between government and private groups, the latter including both nonprofit (voluntary) associations and profit-making firms.[50] This is a relatively recent phenomenon. Services being provided in this manner include a full range of child-care activities: day care, adoption, foster care, group homes, and residential treatment. Other services being provided through contracts are homemaker services for the elderly, family counseling, family planning, services for the developmentally disabled and mentally retarded, and several others.

Major studies have been conducted to determine the extent of use of contracting and intergovernmental contracting in these services,[51] but practically no reports have yet appeared that systematically compare the efficiency and effectiveness of the different service structures. One exception is the study that found that day care was more expensive in government-run centers than in private ones; however, the cost per child went up in private centers when subsidized children were placed there, as a result of (1) quality improvements, (2) increases in wages, and (3) replacement of donated goods and services by purchased goods and services.[52] In other words, cost inflation to government levels and withdrawal of voluntary contributions accounted for much of the increase in cost. Considering the large expenditures for social services, careful comparisons of the relative performance of different arrangements are badly needed and have the potential of leading to large savings of public funds.

PROTECTIVE SERVICES

Private police forces include privately employed guards, investigators, patrolmen, alarm attendants, and armored-car personnel. In 1972 the number of such private police in the United States was more than a half million, and about equal to the number of police in the public law enforcement agencies.[53] In metropolitan areas, private police outnumber the regular police by ratios of two or three to one.

Among the private police are those who work for contract guard services, one of the fastest-growing segments of the industry. Their use is rising at the rate of 10 percent a year, and is epitomized by their use (instead of using regular city police) to guard equipment and property within Boston's City Hall itself. Elsewhere, in Ohio, a specialized private detective agency provided skilled narcotics agents to small-town police departments.[54] The General Services Administration makes extensive use of contract guard services, using them to supply 41 percent of their needs.[55]

The duties of private and public police are vastly different, in the aggregate, but for the narrow function of deterrence by patrol they can be compared, at least with respect to cost if not effectiveness. In 1976, in New York City, contract guards could be procured at a total cost of $4 to $7 per hour, whereas the remuneration alone of a regular police officer, including all fringe benefits but not including any overhead costs, was about $15 per hour.

MISCELLANEOUS SERVICES

Little hard evidence is available on other services. What little evidence exists is localized, shedding light on a particular situation at a particular time. Nevertheless, despite the fact that no general conclusions can be drawn regarding the relative merits of one organizational arrangement over another, it is useful to present whatever scattered reports have come forth, if only to provide food for thought.

Custodial Services

The schools in New York were examined by the City Comptroller, who concluded that large sums of money were being wasted on custodial services. Changing to outside contractors at five schools brought about savings of 13.4 percent and provided a yardstick for evaluating the efficiency of custodial services in the other schools. The comptroller went on to recommend a gradual expansion of the number of schools using outside contactors for such work.[56]

Testimony at a congressional hearing disclosed that at the U.S. Air Force Academy contracting for custodial services instead of providing them by in-house personnel would save $86,000 in three years, and contracting for housekeeping services at the base hospital would save $33,000 over a similar period.[57]

The General Services Agency reports that in the space it controls it contracts for 35 percent of the cleaning and 26 percent of the mechanical maintenance. Moreover, it expects to continue its trend toward contracting for these services.[58] This is an important policy position.

Information is also available on custodial services in Germany. Blankart reports that office cleaning by the federal post office administration is 42 percent to 66 percent more expensive than contracting out, and that the cost of cleaning government offices in Hamburg is 30 percent to 80 percent less costly when done by contract firms.[59]

Food Service

Institutional feeding is a large business in the United States, with an estimated $43 billion being spent annually at workplaces, in health-care institutions, and in educational institutions. About half of this work is done by companies under contract, and the rest by the institution itself using its own employees. Profit margins are small, typically averaging a 2 to 8 percent rate of return before taxes.[60] There would seem to be much room for competition in this field, and indeed a comparative cost analysis of food service at Lowery Air Force Base resulted in an award of a contract to provide the service, at a saving of $1.6 million over three years. A similar evaluation at the airmen's dining hall at the Air Force Academy led to a similar action and a saving of half a million dollars.[61]

Wholesale Markets

Historically in New York, the municipal government had operated food markets where most of the produce brought into the city was sold to wholesalers who then distributed it to retail stores throughout the city. Operation of these markets was shed to the private sector in 1973 and the city realized a net gain in rents and taxes of close to a million dollars.[62]

Tree Trimming

In Detroit, part of the responsibility for trimming healthy trees and removing dead and diseased trees from city streets is contracted to private firms, after a study showed that they could do the work at one-third the unit cost of the city agency.[63]

Forestry

Blankart reports a study in Germany that compared the management of public and private forests.[64] In terms of net operating revenue, the public forests operated at a loss of 30 DM per hectare, whereas the private forests showed a gain of 15 DM per hectare.

Towing

In New York City, a car that is illegally parked in certain areas is subject to being towed away, whereupon a substantial towing fee as well as a parking ticket must be paid by the owner to reclaim his car. The towing was done by a special unit of the police department, and the cost was estimated at $65 per car. Part of the work was subsequently put up for bids, and a contract was awarded to the low bidder, whose price was only $30 per car. (The only other bidder submitted a price of $34.75 per car.)[65]

Data Processing

Orange County, California, the seventh largest county in the nation, contracted with a private firm to manage and operate the county's data processing center and develop new computer programs. By doing this, the county estimated that it would save $12 million, or 30 percent of the cost of continuing to do the work in-house.[66]

A study of the data processing department in a New York City agency showed the productivity of its in-house key punching, generously estimated at 4,400 keystrokes per operator per hour, to be far less than the 8,000 of an average commercial operator and the 10,000 of a good one.

Weather Forecasting

One of the most public of all services is weather forecasting. What is not widely realized, however, is that there are many private firms that offer specialized weather predictions for their clients, and in 1978 rivalry between private weather forecasters and the official National Weather Service broke into the open. Based on a sample of three snowstorms, one of which was correctly predicted by a private service four days before the government predicted it, the private sector claimed credit for superior performance.[67]

An examination of data compiled by the General Accounting Office on the relative efficiency of public and private weather forecasting, ship repair, and bill collection led the researchers to conclude that public-sector costs were two or three times as large as private-sector costs.[68]

Water Supply

An econometric analysis of public and private water companies provided strong evidence that the public agencies had higher operating costs than the private firms.[69]

Legal Aid

A study of legal aid services revealed that poor defendants thought that privately retained lawyers (market arrangement) did the best job, and that court-appointed lawyers (contract service) were inferior. However, the legal community rated the quality equal, and an analysis of conviction and imprisonment rates supported their view: Private and contract lawyers did just as well for their clients and, in fact, the small differences found favored the contract (court-appointed) lawyers.[70]

Other Services

A study by the General Accounting Office (GAO) of government laundry and dry cleaning in federal installations showed that in seven of sixteen cases the cost of in-house operation was greater than the cost of comparable contract service. Thus, in the majority of cases in-house service was at least as efficient as a contractor would be. However, a representative of a private laundry complained that he was unable to find out what the laundering requirements were so that he could prepare a sensible bid to do the work; all he was told was that 246,584 pieces had to be done, and it was impossible for him to learn how many pieces had to be washed, how many to be pressed, and how many, such as towels, merely had to be fluffed dry without ironing.[71]

In another study, it was reported that the GAO examined support services at domestic military installations and concluded that at 22 of the 27 bases the services would have been less costly—by $3.7 million—if the work had been done by contractors. As a result, the GAO recommended more extensive contracting of such activities. This finding is supported by a RAND study that compared support services at two similar air force bases in the Southwest. As measured by the availability of parts and planes, the one serviced by a contractor had better quality and more responsive support than the one ser-

viced by air force civilian employees, while using only 74 percent as much manpower and costing only 87 percent as much
as the latter.[72]

Davies examined government and private banks in Australia and found that managers of government banks hold a higher proportion of their assets in low-risk and low-paying invest-
ments than do their private counterparts. Furthermore, they
arrange easier, less arduous business lives, monitor and orga-
nize work and workers less effectively than do private managers, and have larger staffs. The result is substantially higher
costs in government banks, and a significantly lower rate of return on sales and on capital than in private banks.[73]

Two final examples of contracting for services: The City of
San Francisco hired a private accounting firm to perform some
of the work of its Budget Bureau and saved $102,000 annual-
ly.[74] Detroit hired a private firm to process parking tickets
(which carry fines of $15), at a cost of $1.80 per ticket, after
calculating that it cost $26 per ticket when the city did the
work.[75]

One additional piece of evidence can be cited on the relative
cost of the public and private work force: A study by the Bureau of Labor Statistics showed that in 1974 the benefits of federal employees were 27 percent greater than those of private-
sector nonagricultural employees.[76]

CONCLUSION

It is evident that with few exceptions, little rigorous research
has been done to evaluate and compare public and private provision of services. Nevertheless, the few robust studies cited
above indicate that private provision is superior to public provision of these services. Additional, comprehensive, cross-sec-
tional studies are needed for other services, but they are very
expensive to conduct because they require large sample sizes
and on-site data collection, the latter to ensure comparability

of data. In the absence of such detailed investigations, the available evidence is frequently based on relatively simple statistical tabulations, in which it is assumed — often erroneously — that all other variations are canceled out, and the only difference being observed is that due to public or private operation. In addition, numerous reports of particular examinations are often presented as evidence, but it is difficult to make much of these examples because they are vulnerable to counterexamples.

Nevertheless, while no universal and generalizable conclusion can be drawn from the evidence presented in this chapter, it is safe to say, at the least, that public provision of services is not superior to private provision, while those who believe on a priori grounds that private services are best can find considerable support for their position.

NOTES

1. Lyle C. Fitch, "Increasing the Role of the Private Sector in Providing Public Services," in *Improving the Quality of Urban Management,* ed. Willis D. Hawley and David Rogers (Beverly Hills, Calif.: Sage, 1974), pp. 501-59.
2. John D. Hanrahan, *Government for Sale: Contracting Out, the New Patronage* (Washington, D.C.: American Federation of State, County, and Municipal Employees, 1977).
3. Charles B. Blankart, "Bureaucratic Problems in Public Choice: Why Do Public Goods Still Remain Public?" in *Public Finance and Public Choice,* ed. K.W. Roskamp (Paris: Cujas Publishers, 1979); Robert M. Spann, "Public Versus Private Provision of Governmental Services," in *Budgets and Bureaucrats: The Sources of Government Growth,* ed. Thomas E. Borcherding (Durham, N.C.: Duke University Press, 1977), p. 82; Thomas E. Borcherding, "Toward a Positive Theory of Public Sector Supply Arrangements," Discussion Paper 79-15-3, Department of Economics, Simon Fraser University, British Columbia, Canada, 1979.
4. E.S. Savas, "Public vs. Private Refuse Collection: A Critical Review of the Evidence," *Journal of Urban Analysis* 6 (1979): 1-13.

5. E.S. Savas, "Policy Analysis for Local Government: Public vs. Private Refuse Collection," *Policy Analysis* 3, no. 1 (Winter 1977): 49-74.

6. E.S. Savas, "How Much Do Government Services Really Cost?" *Urban Affairs Quarterly* 15, no. 1 (September 1979): 23-41.

7. "New Orleans Hauler Makes Inroads with Competitive Pricing," *Solid Wastes Management* 20, no. 5 (May 1977): 32-34, 130; "Oklahoma City Three-Way Split," *Solid Wastes Management* 21, no. 3 (March 1978): 42-44, 86; Peter E. Heidenreich, "Public Versus Private Solid Waste Management: The Nashville Approach," *Solid Wastes Management* 21, no. 5 (May 1978): 60-62; Ronald Smothers, "City, as Test, to Seek Bids on Private Refuse Pickup," *New York Times,* 26 March 1980, p. B1.

8. R.A. Meyer, "Publicly Owned Versus Privately Owned Utilities: A Policy Choice," *Review of Economics and Statistics* 57, no. 4 (1975): 391-99.

9. P.C. Mann and J.L. Mikesell, "Ownership and Water Systems Operations," *Water Works Bulletin,* October 1976.

10. R.L. Wallace and P.E. Junk, "Economic Inefficiency of Small Municipal Electric Generating Systems," *Land Economics* 46 (February 1970): 98-104.

11. James A. Yunker, "Economic Performance of Public and Private Enterprise: The Case of U.S. Electric Utilities," *Journal of Economics and Business* 28 (Fall 1975): 60-67; Richard Hellman, *Government Competition in the Electric Utility Industry* (New York: Praeger, 1972). See also Leland G. Neuberg, "Two Issues in the Municipal Ownership of Electric Power Distribution Systems," *Bell Journal of Economics* 8, no. 1 (Spring 1977): 303-23.

12. Sam Peltzman, "Pricing in Public and Private Enterprises: Electric Utilities in the United States," *Journal of Law and Economics* 14 (April 1971): 109-47.

13. Spann, "Public Versus Private Provision."

14. Hellman, *Government Competition in Electric Utility.*

15. Louis DeAlessi, "An Economic Analysis of Government Ownership and Regulation: Theory and the Evidence from the Electric Power Industry," *Public Choice* 19 (Fall 1974): 1-42.

16. Roger S. Ahlbrandt, Jr., *Municipal Fire Protection Services: Comparison of Alternative Organizational Forms* (Beverly Hills, Calif.: Sage, 1973), p. 45.
17. Mark Frazier, "Scottsdale Slashes Spending," *Reader's Digest,* February 1978.
18. David Gilman, "Can Private Enterprise Deliver the Public Goods?" *Dun and Bradstreet Reports Magazine* 27, no. 1 (January-February 1979): 20-28.
19. Howell Raines, "Officials Face Possible Ouster for Cutting Back Jobs," *New York Times,* 9 February 1979, p. A18.
20. Robert W. Poole, Jr., "Private Fire Departments," *Fiscal Watchdog,* January 1979. National Taxpayers Union, Local Government Center, Santa Barbara, Calif.
21. Gilman, "Can Private Enterprise Deliver?"
22. David G. Davies, "The Efficiency of Public Versus Private Firms, The Case of Australia's Two Airlines," *Journal of Law and Economics* 14, no. 1 (April 1971): 149-65.
23. Blankart, "Bureaucratic Problems."
24. Office of the Comptroller, State of New York, *Summary of Audit Reports on New York City Transit Authority Operations,* Report No. NY-Auth-6-76, 1976.
25. New York State Legislative Commission on Expenditure Review, *Pupil Transportation Programs,* 30 January 1978.
26. Ronald Kessler, "The Great Mail Bungle," *Washington Post,* 12 June 1974; Henry Scott-Stokes, "UPS Shines in Yule Package Service," *New York Times,* 10 December 1977; Ernest Holsendolph, "Mails Losing Package Business," *New York Times,* 30 May 1977.
27. John Haldi, *Postal Monopoly: An Assessment of the Private Express Statutes* (Washington, D.C.: American Enterprise Institute, 1974); Ted Vaden, "Soaring Costs Cloud Postal Service Future," *Congressional Quarterly Weekly Report* 34 (20 March 1976): 627-33; Ernest Holsendolph, "Should U.S. Postal Office Continue as a Monopoly?" *New York Times,* 3 February 1976.
28. Ernest Holsendolph, "Mail Service Competition Rising," *New York Times,* 18 April 1976, p. 31; Cynthia Jabs, "And Deliver Us from the Post Office," *New York Times,* 4 July 1976, sec. 3, p. 2; Philip H. Dougherty, "Alternatives to the Postal Service," *New York Times,* 2 February 1978, p. D11;

"Deliverer Facing Action as Flouter of Postal Law," *New York Times,* 18 April 1976, p. 31; "Mailman Vows He'll Fight On," *Chicago Tribune,* 17 August 1976, sec. 4, p. 13; "Court Stops Mrs. Brennan's Postal Service," *New York Times,* 6 August 1978; Michael S. Larsky, "Alternative Delivery: Is the Postal Service Really Necessary?" *Folio* 2 (February 1973): 34-40.

29. "Agencies Told to Skip Postal Service," *Washington Post,* 21 May 1976.

30. *An Overview of Nursing Home Characteristics: Provisional Data from the 1977 National Nursing Home Survey,* Advance Data No. 35 (Washington, D.C.: U.S. Department of Health, Education, and Welfare, Public Health Service, National Center for Health Statistics, 6 September 1978).

31. Cotton M. Lindsay, *Veterans Administration Hospitals* (Washington, D.C.: American Enterprise Institue, 1975), p. 11.

32. Spann, "Public Versus Private Provision."

33. David P. Garino, "Profits from Patients: Hospitals Discover New Private Ownership Brings More Efficiency — and Controversy," *Wall Street Journal,* 6 January 1972, p. 28; Charles W. Baird, "On Profits and Hospitals," *Journal of Economic Issues* 5 (March 1971): 57-66; Robert W. Poole, Jr., "Curing Sick City Hospitals," *Fiscal Watchdog,* October 1978. National Taxpayers Union, Local Government Center, Santa Barbara, Calif.

34. Richard W. Nathan, "Holding Down Expenditures for Hospital Care in New York City," *City Almanac* 13, no. 3 (October 1978). Center for New York City Affairs, The New School for Social Research.

35. Myron D. Fottler and William C. Rock, "Some Correlates of Hospital Costs in Public and Private Hospital Systems: New York City," *Quarterly Review of Economics and Business* 14 (Spring 1974): 39-53.

36. Hirsch S. Ruchlin, Dennis D. Pointer, and Lloyd L. Cannedy, "A Comparison of For-Profit Investor-Owned Chain and Nonprofit Hospitals," *Inquiry* 10, no. 4 (December 1973): 13-23.

37. Spann, "Public Versus Private Provision."

38. Lindsay, *Veterans Administration Hospitals.*

39. *Comptroller's Report, City of New York* 4, no. 5 (November 1978).
40. William Hsiao, "Public Versus Private Administration of Health Insurance: A Study in Relative Economic Efficiency," *Inquiry* 15 (December 1978): 379-87.
41. H.E. French III, "Health Insurance: Private, Mutuals or Governments," in *Proceedings of the Seminar on the Economics of Nonproprietary Organizations,* ed. K.W. Clarkson and D.L. Martin (Greenwich, Conn.: Jai Press, 1980).
42. Robert L. Ciszewski, *Contraceptive Marketing Program in Bangladesh Doubles Number Practicing Birth Control* (New York: Population Services International, 20 September 1978).
43. John Davies and Terrence D.J. Lavis, "Measuring the Effectiveness of Contraceptive Marketing Programs: Preethi in Sri Lanka," *Studies in Family Planning* 8, no. 4 (April 1977): 82-90.
44. *Policy Analysis of the Cost and Financing of Special Education to Handicapped Children in New York City* (New York: Office of the Comptroller, 22 May 1978).
45. Thomas A. Johnson, "Black-Run Private Schools Lure Growing Numbers in New York," *New York Times,* 5 April 1980, p. 1.
46. John E. Coons and Joseph Kul, "Schools: What's Happening to Local Control?" *Taxing and Spending* 1, no. 1 (October-November 1978): 39.
47. Lena Williams, "Private Universities Held Cost Efficient," *New York Times,* 10 April 1977, p. 27.
48. C. Lowell Harriss, "CUNY, SUNY, and the 'Independents': New Directions for Higher Education in New York City," *City Almanac* 10, no. 4 (December 1975).
49. William Orzechowski, "Economic Models of Bureaucracy: Survey, Extensions, and Evidence," in Borcherding, *Budgets and Bureaucrats,* pp. 229-59.
50. Kenneth R. Wedel, "Government Contracting for Purchase of Service," *Social Work* 21, no. 2 (March 1976): 101-5; Sam Edwards, Bill Benton, Tracy Field, and Rhona Miller, "The Purchase of Service and Title XX," Working Paper 0990-18 (Washington, D.C.: Urban Institute, February 1978).
51. *Title XX Purchase of Service: A Description of States' Deliv-*

ery and Management Practices (Berkeley, Calif.: Pacific Consultants, October 1978).
52. Michael Krashinsky, "The Cost of Day Care in Public Programs," *National Tax Journal* 31, no. 4 (December 1978): 363-72.
53. James S. Kakalik and Sorrel Wildhorn, *The Private Police: Security and Danger* (New York: Crane Russak, 1977).
54. "Rent-a-Narc," *Newsweek*, 27 August 1973, p. 25.
55. Tom L. Peyton, Jr., "Standards for Public Building Maintenance," *APWA Reporter* 44, no. 10 (October 1977): 28-29.
56. Charles Kaiser, "Custodial Services in the Schools Termed Wasteful by Goldin," *New York Times*, 24 January 1977, p. 45.
57. Jack I. Posner, Statement, *Hearings on Contracting Out of Jobs and Services, Subcommittee on Employee Ethics and Utilization, Committee on Post Office and Civil Service*, House of Representatives, Serial No. 95-29 (Washington, D.C.: U.S. Government Printing Office, 1977), p. 14.
58. Peyton, "Standards for Public Building Maintenance."
59. Blankart, "Bureaucratic Problems."
60. Pamela G. Hollie, "Lunch Becomes Big Business," *New York Times*, 19 May 1978, p. D1.
61. Posner, Statement, *Hearings*, pp. 13-14.
62. D. Kenneth Patton, Economic Development Administration, City of New York, letter report dated 21 June 1973.
63. Frederick O'R. Hayes, *Productivity in Local Government* (Lexington, Mass.: Lexington Books, 1977), p. 43.
64. Blankart, "Bureaucratic Problems."
65. Charles Kaiser, "Private Towaways," *New York Times*, 4 September 1976.
66. "Computer Science Corporation to Manage County Systems," *National Civic Review*, January 1974, p. 40.
67. Gregory Jaynes, "Public vs. Private Weathermen," *New York Times*, 15 February 1978.
68. J.T. Bennett and M.J. Johnson, *Federal Government Growth, 1959-78: Theory and Empirical Evidence* (New York: International Center for Economic Policy Studies, 1980).
69. W.M. Crain and A. Zardkooh, "A Test of the Property-Rights Theory of the Firm: Water Utilities in the United States," *Journal of Law and Economics* (October 1978).

70. Robert Hermann, Eric Single, and John Boston, *Counsel for the Poor: Criminal Defense in Urban America* (Lexington, Mass.: Lexington Books, 1977).

71. John Contney, Statement, *Hearings on Contracting Out of Jobs and Services, Part II, Subcommittee on Employee Ethics and Utilization, Committee on Post Office and Civil Service,* House of Representatives, Serial No. 95-29 (Washington, D.C.: U.S. Government Printing Office, 1977), pp. 74-75.

72. Edward C. Leeson, Statement, *Hearings on Contracting Out of Jobs and Services, Part II, Subcommittee on Employee Ethics and Utilization, Committee on Post Office and Civil Service,* House of Representatives, Serial No. 95-29 (Washington, D.C.: U.S. Government Printing Office, 1977), p. 153.

73. David G. Davies, "Property Rights and Economic Behavior in Private and Government Enterprises: The Case of Australia's Banking System" (unpublished manuscript, Duke University, August 1978).

74. "City of San Francisco Contracts Out Budget Bureau Services and Saves $$," *Newsletter, Municipal Finance Officers Association* 54, no. 4 (16 February 1972): 2.

75. Susan Tompor, "For Fast Cash, Cities Pursue Illegal Parkers," *Wall Street Journal,* 23 July 1981, p. 25.

76. Bureau of Labor Statistics, "Employee Compensation in the Professional, Administrative, Technical and Clerical Survey," *Industry Surveys* no. 464 (1975).

CHAPTER 7

TOWARD SENSIBLE GOVERNMENT

The ideas that emerged in the preceding chapters can be applied to halt and reverse the growth of government. Four broad, supplementary, and interrelated strategies may be followed:

1. Some of the goods that have come to be supplied by government in recent years should be allowed to revert to their original status, to be supplied by the marketplace or by voluntary arrangements; this would be achieved by government withdrawal from the service, or "load shedding."
2. Government involvement in service delivery should be reduced by making greater use of those arrangements in which government plays a relatively limited role.
3. User charges should be levied wherever possible.
4. Arrangements that permit competition should be utilized to the maximum feasible extent.

LOAD SHEDDING

The extensive collectivization of goods that were heretofore considered private goods, such as education, health care, housing, income maintenance, and various social services, has resulted in excessive waste and, it can be argued, has failed to achieve reasonable expectations. It is time to pursue other alternatives toward the desired objective of social well-being. Specifically, government's overly dominant role in supplying some of these goods should be diminished gradually. A side benefit of such a step is the prospect that the reduction in government expenditures for these purposes will lead to economic developments that will supply these goods through other arrangements.

For example, many social and health services that have been redefined as collective and common-pool goods and that account for much of the growth in government expenditures are already being delivered through the marketplace, and that mechanism can be strengthened. Private firms typically provide such fringe benefits to their employees as pensions and subsidized life, health, and unemployment insurance. With reduced government involvement in such services, the list of employer-provided fringe benefits could be extended to include housing, education, and day care for young and aged dependents of the employee, in each case utilizing nongovernmental service-delivery arrangements. The cost of this expanded fringe-benefit package would be offset by lower taxes and, depending on the size and composition of the package, by lower wages. Ideally, employees should be free to choose either these fringe benefits or cash, but changes in the tax laws will be needed to avoid penalizing employees who take advantage of the option to "cash in" their fringe benefits.

Day care is a promising candidate for load shedding. Since time immemorial, parents have arranged for relatives, friends, and neighbors to care for their children; and parents have taken into consideration the character and qualities of the individual to whom they've entrusted their children and the conditions of the surroundings in which their children will be placed. In recent years, however, day care has become the object of increasing government involvement and financing. The result has been an increasingly complex web of legal restrictions as to who can provide the service, the number and kind of personnel who must be in attendance, the nature of the facilities, and so forth, with the bizarre result that most families and homes today would not be approved by government as suitable for child care.

If government withdraws from this newly created government service, voluntary arrangements will surely reemerge and expand to fill the need. One can even imagine McDonald's starting a franchised day-care business. More broadly, the family should be restored once again to its historic position as the principal decision-making unit with respect to health, education, and welfare and the principal arranger of these desired services. We have government-financed child day-care centers and government-financed senior-citizen centers, with middle-aged people working in each. There would seem to be room for imaginative merging of the two kinds of services in some way and, to some extent, to replicate the age-old practice of the old caring for the young.

Government withdrawal from such services will not be easy, for a new political consensus must be achieved to replace the older one that brought about collectivization and government entry in the first place. The swelling discontent with the size, growth, and overbearing presence of government suggests that at last it may be possible to create that consensus.

This need not involve a bruising battle between opposing ideologies. All that is needed is appropriate encouragement of natural forces that are already at work and producing movement, however modest, in the described direction with respect to particular services. For an illustration, one can look at municipal tennis courts in New York City. Dissatisfaction with their condition led many players to abandon the city facilities in favor of private ones and ultimately helped persuade the city to lease its courts to private operators; that is, to switch from municipal to franchise service.

Gradual or partial load shedding can be carried out for a whole range of recreational activities besides tennis, such as golf and swimming. Publicly owned facilities could be sold off to private bidders and operated as ordinary private businesses selling their services to the public at large, or functioning as nonprofit membership organizations that are prohibited from engaging in discriminatory practices. The rationale for doing so is that these specialized recreational pursuits are classical toll goods, exclusion of nonpayers is possible, and the benefits accrue directly to the users with little spillover to society at large. There is little reason for government to provide these goods at collective expense, and every reason for the aficionados to band together for mutual enjoyment under their own rules and at their own expense.

We may be seeing the early stages of a similar phenomenon in public education in large cities. Even parents of limited means have been withdrawing their children from the public schools in droves and enrolling them in private schools. This reduction in demand invites load shedding. Policies that would treat this trend as an opportunity are discussed later in this chapter.

Load shedding can also take place through the voluntary formation of geographic collective units, in both urban and suburban communities. Virtually unnoticed, a brand new, very local level of government is emerging in this country — the condominium. It has great potential. Condominiums, neighborhood organizations and civic associations — we can call them "voluntary micro collectives" — can assume the responsibility for social services, cleaning and maintaining streets and local parks, removing snow, collecting refuse, and operating voluntary ambulance, fire, and patrol services, as appropriate. Such organizations can forge a desperately needed sense of community and can restore citizenship skills that have atrophied from disuse, skills without which a democracy cannot long survive.

Such units can best be formed in established communities that have well-defined geographic boundaries, are relatively homogeneous in terms of income, and have shared values with respect to the services to be provided through this mechanism. Local leadership is necessary, as is an encouraging posture by the local government. This latter can best be made manifest by providing tax rebates to residents in units that forego the erstwhile city services. This poses a minor administrative problem for the local government, but many communities do this, including Houston and Kansas City. Another device to encourage the creation and assure the viability of such self-governing associations is to grant them taxing authority as special assessment districts. The State of New York has passed legislation to make this possible.

Seen in this light, at the same time that government has been growing, load shedding has been proceeding—without overt political struggles—as a minor countercurrent. The demand for certain collective goods has exceeded the ability of government to supply them at a suitable price, particularly in cities that have been experiencing fiscal stress and high costs of public services. Many municipal services have declined in quantity and quality to the point where exasperated citizens have formed organizations to supplement the municipal service. In New York, for example, citizen safety patrols have been organized and groups of neighborhood merchants have formed associations that take on tasks such as cleaning sidewalks and streets and maintaining greenery. Other groups have formed to undertake maintenance and restoration work in Central Park and elsewhere. In London and Seattle similar local efforts are encouraged by policies that permit the city governments to contract with such voluntary groups to assume this responsibility at a cost that is far lower than the city would pay for municipal service. From the standpoint of these voluntary associations, they obtain the services they want, custom-tailored to their specific local needs and preferences; they exert a direct influence over the quality of their surroundings, pay less than they would otherwise, and their members have a chance to contribute their labor instead of their money. (In the days of a barter economy, people could pay their taxes in specie such as grain and livestock. In a market economy they must pay cash. Load shedding can be said to restore to the taxpayer the opportunity to pay in kind — with his labor. "Off the books" earnings would then have their counterpart in "off the books" tax payments, that is, payments in kind for collective goods.)

To summarize more precisely, alternative arrangements have emerged to supply services that the government arrangement was not supplying satisfactorily. To implement load shedding, then, can involve no more than a no-growth policy for government and natural growth for the alternative arrangements. Limiting devices such as Proposition 13, spending caps, budget cuts, revenue cuts, revenue limitations, and mandatory balanced budgets all facilitate this process. Inflation can actually help to the extent that limitations are applied in absolute dollar amounts. More vigorous pursuit of load shedding involves encouraging the growth of these alternative arrangements by offering tax rebates, issuing vouchers, conferring assessment authority on the above-mentioned micro collectives, and contracting with local citizen groups.

A systematic review of government-supplied goods and services, to see which ones can revert — admittedly with much effort — to private or toll goods, and which collective goods might be supplied by voluntary arrangements, might be criticized on the grounds that the ax will fall on the poor, for they are the principal beneficiaries of government action. This need not be the case. In the first place, the poor could be served even better by the marketplace if they were given vouchers or a negative income tax. Second, it is primarily the broad middle class that pays for government programs and is the main beneficiary, although this is not to say that the process is therefore fair and benign. In the main, taxes are taken from powerless middle-class *individuals* and given to organized middle-class *groups*. Government intervenes to create a carefully crafted set

of beneficiaries — be they tobacco growers, veterans, construction workers, day-care users, the elderly, the auto industry, or
lawyers — while pocketing a substantial portion of the tax dollar to pay for the expense of considering and identifying the
potential beneficiaries and figuring out how to direct the taxpayers' money to them. Indeed, one might say with only mod-
erate exaggeration that much of the government's revenue
goes to pay for the expense of making and executing decisions
about redistributing the remainder of the revenues back to
middle-class taxpayers in the form of government-produced
services. The taxpayer would be better off if he were free to
keep more of his income and decide for himself what to buy
with it, rather than to get back only a portion of it after lobby-
ing as a member of a group, and getting it in a less satisfying,
less useful, and possibly unwanted form — all the while being
expected to feel grateful for the beneficence of his elected representatives.

LIMITED-GOVERNMENT ARRANGEMENTS

The second broad strategy cited above for restraining the size
of government is to make greater use of those arrangements in
which government plays a more limited role in service delivery. That is, institutional arrangements should be chosen so
that government is involved in only a minimal way or not at
all. By this rule one would prefer market arrangements for private goods (e.g., private day-care facilities), market or franchise arrangements for toll goods (e.g., lease or sale of municipal utilities such as water supply, and recreational facilities
such as tennis courts), and voluntary service for collective
goods (e.g., ambulance service in small communities). If it is
decided that the cost of a service is to be paid collectively, then
a government subsidy through a grant or voucher system is
preferred over direct government service. (A firm believer in
citizen choice might argue against the paternalism of choice-

directing grants and vouchers and would call instead for a negative income tax, thereby providing poor citizens with both
the wherewithal and the freedom to purchase the goods they
desire. However, protectors of the public interest would no
doubt find that poor people's preferences are insufficiently re-
fined and their expenditures thoughtlessly shortsighted, and
therefore would hasten to appoint guardians to establish family budgets and supervise spending.)

The preferred rankings of alternative institutional structures, for each type of good, appear in table 7.1. The basic
principle used to produce these rankings is simply the relative
size of government expenditures: the lower the cost to be paid
out of taxes, the higher the ranking.

TABLE 7.1

*Ranking of Institutional Arrangements to Reduce
Government Expenditures, by Type of Good*

Arrangement	Private Goods	Toll Goods	Collective Goods	Common-Pool Goods
Self-service	1			
Voluntary		1	1	1
Market	2	2		
Franchise		3		
Voucher	3	4		2
Grant	3	4		2
Contract		6	2	4
Intergovernmental contract		7	3	5
Government service		8	4	6

NOTE: The highest ranking is 1.

It is instructive to look at housing to see how measures to reduce the role of government might work. Housing has been
the object of greatly expanded government attention. Publicly
run housing, government grants for housing construction,
government mortgages, and rent control have all grown enor-
mously. Housing allowances for tenants—a form of voucher
—are being used. Federal housing funds are even used to pay

for clinics that advise people of the importance of paying their
rents and teach them the virtues of household budgeting to
make sure they are able to do so. Perhaps the ultimate in government involvement in housing was achieved by the enter-
prising mayor on Long Island who was able to obtain a special
subsidy from the U.S. Department of Housing and Urban Development to paint the exteriors of houses owned by eligible
homeowners in his community. Apparently the judgment was
made that, to a significant degree, a well-painted house is a
collective good and merits a public subsidy.[1] Presumably, the
collective good involved is that a passerby who happens to
glance in that direction will have a beautiful experience instead
of having his aesthetic sense assailed by an unpainted house.
But what if the color is not to his liking? Why not a collective
decision on acceptable and desired colors? By the same reasoning that implicitly pronounces house painting to be a collective
good, why not more attractive clothing, modish hair styling,
and face lifts for all, at collective expense?

In New York City, about half the housing stock has come
under government control in one way or another, by tax fore-
closure, imposition of rent control, granting of subsidies and
tax abatements, and construction of public housing. The effect
of this large-scale intervention by government has not been a
noteworthy success. In fact, although it may be unfair to attribute all of New York's housing ills to these policies, the results are well known: abandonment of structurally sound
buildings, destruction of neighborhoods, and the prevalence
of slums — with the city itself as the nation's biggest and most
notorious slumlord, owning and operating far and away the
largest number of slum dwellings.

Rent control was established shortly after World War II because of a temporary shortage of housing. By what line of reasoning price controls might have been expected to increase the
supply of housing remains obscure. Nevertheless, rent control
has been retained and expanded on the grounds that the hous-

ing shortage persists unabated to this day. Evidence that purports to show this alleged shortage is based on the observed vacancy rate. However, the rate calculation excludes empty, abandoned units! What is more, citing a 5 percent vacancy rate as evidence of a housing shortage is somewhat akin to declaring a hot-dog shortage unless the number grilled is substantially greater than the number eaten.

The construction of a great deal of government and government-subsidized housing, combined with the loss of population and the inability of owners to earn an adequate income due to rent control, goes far to explain why so many housing units have been abandoned in New York.

While abandonment has proceeded apace, spurred by myopic government policies, the construction of government-aided housing has also gone on, with equally unfortunate results. As an example, the favored, middle-class tenants of Co-op City, an immense, publicly assisted housing project in the Bronx, banded together and exerted their considerable political pressure to avoid paying the full costs of their housing, thereby taxing their fellow citizens—most of whom have lower incomes—to foot their housing bill. That this is not an isolated occurrence is indicated by the State Comptroller's warning that by 1983 only 4 out of 113 state-assisted housing projects will be in the black, although all of them were designed to generate sufficient rental revenue to meet current operating expenses and low-interest mortgage payments.[2] The tenants do not want to pay even the subsidized cost of their housing; political leaders are loathe to force them to do so; and since the state in effect guaranteed the mortgage, the state is left holding the bag and using taxes to cover the difference. Again, a government service has led to the creation of an organized group that benefits uniquely from that service and is able to use political power to extract more benefits from the society at large.

Given the enormous distortions that have occurred in New York's housing arena since large-scale deviation from market operations first occurred, the future may seem bleak. Nevertheless, signs of economic rationality, however bizarre, are beginning to reappear. The city, falling heir to more and more buildings because of tax arrears, found that it, too, was unable to operate the properties except at a loss, even though the city doesn't have to pay taxes on these newly acquired properties the way the former owners were supposed to. Thereupon, the city promptly passed a law eliminating rent control on its buildings, thus enabling it to auction the housing on the open market at higher prices than it would otherwise get. This pragmatic approach is thoroughly inequitable because it amounts to simple expropriation of property, but at least it represents belated recognition that the market is an appropriate way to provide housing.

The move toward the marketplace in New York can be aided by changing a particularly mangled form of rent voucher, namely, the rent supplement given to welfare recipients. Instead of including a predetermined allowance for housing in the regular monthly welfare check, or at least giving a rent voucher in a fixed dollar amount to each welfare family, the rent supplement is treated separately and given to the welfare recipient to pay the going rent in the building he or she happens to inhabit. Thus, two families that are otherwise in equal circumstances may receive drastically different rent allowances depending on where each has chosen to live. Such unequal treatment is inherently unfair; just as food and clothing allowances are calculated according to a standard formula, the housing allowance should be handled the same way, and each family should start on an equal footing. Using a true voucher, or better yet, cash, it should purchase its housing in the open market. (Nevertheless, one should note that an experiment involving a direct cash subsidy to low-income families revealed a marked indifference to the program. Families were generally satisfied with their housing and did not want to receive and spend more money for better housing.[3] In effect, households wanted less housing than government bureaucrats thought they should have.)

Public housing projects, designed as warehouses for the poor, or so some would say, often concentrate problem families in a small area, in many cases destroying that neighborhood. Again, it would be better to provide housing vouchers and let the marketplace bring about a match between dwellings and tenants, thereby providing more freedom of choice to low-income families and reducing the cost to the taxpayer by selling off inefficiently run public housing. (When a judge placed Boston's Housing Authority in receivership, as noted in chapter 5, he accused the directors—who are appointed by the mayor and governor—of "gross mismanagement, nonfeasance, incompetence and irresponsibility."[4]) If this were done, it is likely that housing which would otherwise be abandoned would be occupied and saved, while public housing would lose some of its clientele, just as county and municipal hospitals lost theirs when low-income families were granted, through Medicaid, freedom of choice in health care.

Despite all this government intervention in the housing market, Professor Drucker points out that it is the private sector that developed the first truly low-cost housing in history: the mobile home.[5] Nine-tenths of low-priced homes, which comprise a third of the total market, are mobile homes. (Of course, once placed on concrete slabs they are as immobile as conventional houses.) In short, the free market has shown a promising path; mobile homes (*manufactured* homes, if you please, in industry's parlance) are the best solution so far to the problem of building low-cost housing. If local governments were to adopt more reasonable zoning and building codes, it is safe to predict that the mobile-home industry would grow and develop, attract capital, conduct the research necessary to improve its products further, and design and build attractive communities of salable houses. The result would be a far cry from the infamous Pruit-Igoe project in St. Louis, which stood briefly at

the nadir of government housing before it was mercifully de-
molished in the public interest.

There is yet another area of the housing field where a different method of providing service can bring about a major improvement. Building codes are imposed by city governments
with the intent of assuring public safety. In fact, their dominant effect is to force residents to pay for costly and archaic
construction techniques, featherbedding, and corrupt inspectors. The National Commission on Neighborhoods found that
building codes in the United States add significantly to the cost
of rehabilitation and recommended features of the system used
in France:

1. A code for safety-related matters
2. Performance-based guidelines for construction
3. Liability of contractors for building components and construction

If this were done in the United States, one could anticipate
that, as in France, safe construction would be enforced by the
marketplace as builders purchase insurance to protect themselves against claims, insurance companies hire inspection
firms, and banks make building loans preferentially to insured
builders.[6] Economic pressures may yet bring about such
changes.

In principle, people should be required to pay the full cost of
their housing, for they are the personal beneficiaries of this in-
dubitably private good. Cities should gradually move toward
the elimination of rent controls, indirect subsidies, and tax
abatements and slowly divest themselves of troubled public
housing, while using housing vouchers for the indigent. The
result of these actions would be that low-income residents
would not have to support the middle class in Co-op City and
similar housing projects, and the middle class would pay the
full cost of heretofore rent-controlled and rent-stabilized
apartments; at the same time, if government-aided featherbed-

ding in the construction industries were ended, it is likely that the marketplace would reassume its long-established position as the principal provider of suitable housing for all. After all, it worked this way for the first three hundred years of American urban history and succeeded in absorbing huge waves of penniless immigrants around the turn of this century.

This will not be easy to bring about. Nevertheless, the spiraling cost of home heating is forcing cities to relax overly stringent rent-control laws. At the same time, the desire to provide low-cost housing to senior citizens through rent control means that serious inequities are appearing in multiple dwellings, where younger people pay far more than older people for identical apartments in the same building. This may set the stage for a coalition of landlords, full-price renters in private housing, and low-income tenants in public housing to press for reforms in the system.

An even more promising trend is the move to convert privately owned multiple dwellings to cooperative ownership, in which case rent control is automatically ended. The process can be thought of as reducing the number of tenants and increasing the number of landlords, thereby achieving a better political balance between these two natural enemies and easing the selfish, tenant-powered demand for continuation of rent controls.

USER CHARGES

The third strategy identified at the outset of this chapter as an approach to limiting the size of government is the imposition of user charges wherever practicable. This should be done for all private and toll goods provided directly by government, by intergovernmental agreement, and by contract arrangements. The fundamental purpose of the user charge in this context is not so much to raise money but rather to reveal fully the true cost of service, thereby creating the possibility and, therefore, the opportunity of making comparisons and devising alternatives.

It may be argued that a user charge is antithetical to the notion of limiting government, for it is merely another method for collecting funds to be expended by government. This is faulty and short-sighted reasoning. A service financed by a user charge should be compared to a service financed by taxes, both of which are provided by the same delivery arrangement. The cost of the latter is obscured, but the cost of the former is highly visible. If hidden subsidies for government-produced services are prohibited, and the full cost of service is charged to the user, citizens will start looking for alternatives if they feel the service isn't worth the price. This situation arose in St. Paul, Minnesota, where both the city and the private sector sold residential refuse collection service; the city's cost was 26 percent higher than that of most private firms, and the city lost virtually all its customers except for senior citizens and welfare recipients, who were eligible to receive city service at half price.

It is somewhat surprising that user charges are not used more widely for government services in the United States. One might expect that toll goods, such as refuse collection in densely populated cities, would be paid for entirely out of taxes in socialist countries and in Western European countries ruled by social democrats. Surprisingly, that is not the case. In Vienna, Belgrade, and Moscow, citizens pay a monthly charge for that service; in the United States, San Francisco is one of the few large cities where residents pay a fee for service.

Political leaders seem to find irresistible the notion of eliminating user charges and providing a service "free" to their constituents, that is, paying for it out of taxes that are hidden from view. Consider the allegory of the engineer, the economist, and the state senator sitting in a rowboat near New York City's George Washington Bridge and observing the rush-hour traffic. The engineer wants to enlarge the bridge to relieve congestion. The economist wants to increase the existing toll and introduce time-of-day pricing to reduce peak-hour usage. But the state senator starts drafting a bill to eliminate the toll altogether and anticipates with barely concealed glee the boundless gratitude that all those motorists will feel toward him at election time.

What is the likelihood that user charges will become more commonplace? Very good. Proposition 13 in California, tax limitations elsewhere, and "spending caps" in various jurisdictions are resulting in greater use of such charges, for they are not taxes and are generally outside the purview of these revenue-limiting devices.

There are administrative costs involved in collecting user charges; for example, procedures for billing and for handling delinquent accounts must be established. Furthermore, while the charge is theoretically applicable to all private and toll goods, it is more appropriate for some than for others. Consider water supply and refuse collection as contrasting examples. Water can be turned off to a delinquent account with no harm to the neighbors, but a similar sanction involving refuse collection would result in a neighborhood nuisance. User charges work best when the service involves no external side effects on others and exclusion is a relatively simple matter, as in turning off gas or water or prohibiting a delinquent borrower from checking another book out of the public library.

Gaining political acceptability of any new charge is always a problem, of course, but the more clearly the service is a private or a toll good, with individual, identifiable beneficiaries, and the more that service is permitted to deteriorate due to underfinancing, the more acceptable a user charge becomes, like an increase in mass-transit fares.

COMPETITION

Government growth will not yield to preaching, indignation,

or finger-pointing at villains. The forces of competition must be brought to bear, even though competition, too, has limitations.[7] The failure to understand the distinction between *providing for* a service and *producing* the service has led to a curious reliance on monopoly mechanisms for delivering public services. How strange. We are vigorously opposed to monopolies in the private sector and enforce laws to break up monopolies and conspiracies that would restrain competition; we know that the public interest suffers without the goad of competition and in the absence of alternative choices. But in the public sector, perversely, we have often chosen monopoly and prohibited competition in the mistaken belief that competition constitutes wasteful duplication. We labor under the enormous delusion that total reliance on a single supplier is the best way to assure satisfactory delivery of vital public services if the supplier is the government itself.

Hence, in improving government services the emphasis has been on better public administration, preservice education, inservice training, civil service reform, budgeting reforms, computers, quantitative methods, reorganization, organizational development, incentive systems, productivity programs, joint labor-management committees, and the like. All of these are desirable, but they fail to identify, let alone address, the underlying, structural problem of government monopolies.

Introducing competition requires a conscious strategy of creating alternatives and fostering a receptive climate and mental attitude in favor of giving options to the citizen-consumers of public services.[8] Service delivery options are essential. Total dependence on a single supplier, whether a government agency or a private firm, is dangerous. Without choice and flexibility the consumer of public services, the citizen, is subject to endless exploitation and victimization. He and his government should have a chance to shop around, for when choice is replaced by compulsion, the fundamental relationship between citizens and public employees is drastically altered; there are no public servants any more.

The existence of public service options provides a form of insurance; if several organizations are delivering the same service and one fails or is subject to too many work stoppages, or is inefficient, or ineffective, or unresponsive, or unsatisfactory, or too expensive, the public can turn to another supplier. Furthermore, separating the decision about supplying a service—what kind, what quality, how much—from the actual production process gives the citizen-consumer greater leverage and liberates him from the control of a single bureaucracy that determines what service he will get, how much of it he will consume, how it will be produced, and how much he will pay for it.

Such monopoly power has important consequences. When a service is financed by taxes without pricing and without citizen choice, there is no effective way to determine the level of popular support for the service except in the very long term. Ordinarily, customers who have a choice will seek out producers who will tailor their services to satisfy their customers' different needs. Citizens who are denied the right to choose one alternative over another cannot indicate their preferences to shape the service, and the ballot box is a poor substitute for communicating program preferences. In the absence of citizen choice, so-called public servants have a captive market and little incentive to heed their putative customers. Control of the service depends instead on the relative political power of the interested parties.

Competition can be fostered between different producers within the same or different institutional arrangements. For example, a civilian advisory board has called for competitive analysis of intelligence information to reduce the monopolistic role of the Central Intelligence Agency in this function. The French government, unwilling to end the state monopoly of television, nevertheless responded to complaints about its "incompetent, flippant, disjointed and criminally wasteful" Office of French Radio and Television with a decision to establish each of the three channels as a completely independent, competing, government institution.[9]

A refreshing and thought-provoking example of a deliberate effort to stimulate intergovernmental competition comes from Yugoslavia. The city fathers of Ljubljana, the capital of Slovenia, desired the services of some city planners and solicited formal bids not only from the city planning agency of their city but also from the city planning agency of Zagreb, the capital of the neighboring Croatian Republic. An American observer there at the time remarked that he had never seen city employees anywhere work as hard as Ljubljana's city planners, who wanted desperately to avoid the humiliation of having their own city's work contracted out to their professional and regional rivals.[10]

Nowhere is the problem of monopoly more serious and competition more needed than in education. Primary and secondary education is the largest function of state and local government, as measured by the size of the budget and the number of employees. In large cities, most students are below the national average in reading and mathematics. Teachers attribute the problem to conditions in the home. Parents blame uncaring teachers. The education establishment wants more money spent on the problem. No one has a certain prescription for teaching inner-city children.

What should you do when you don't know what to do? The answer: Do many different things. Nature's incessant experimentation with mutations enables species to evolve, adapt, and survive despite drastic environmental changes; some of these "experiments" turn out to be better suited to the new surroundings than the original model and ultimately replace it. Similarly, a variety of educational approaches should be encouraged to see which ones can prove themselves fit and able to educate the city's children. Today's monolithic public school system is inadequate, yet it cannot effectively facilitate broad experimentation or tolerate alternative pedagogical approaches. Diversity has never been the strong suit of government. The education of millions of children is stunted and the effort of many dedicated teachers is wasted by the traditional and blind iṇ̣sistence on a government education monopoly. "Education which truly meets the needs of the public can be achieved only by allowing the public free choice to sample, judge, and individually vote for the education they choose."[11]

The government monopoly is particularly stifling in that, for the most part, pupils must attend a particular school; generally they are not free even to attend another school within the monopoly. Clearly such a policy is designed for the administrative convenience of the school system rather than the educational advantage of the child.

The ultimate in governmental education monopoly was attempted in Oregon. A 1922 state law, subsequently overturned by the U.S. Supreme Court, outlawed all private schools and compelled all children to attend government schools. Interestingly enough, the motive force behind the passage of this law was the Ku Klux Klan, with its fear of foreign influences.[12]

A comparison of ancient Athens and Sparta with respect to education monopolies is instructive. In Sparta there was no scope for parental choice. The state's responsibility went so far as to remove children from their homes and place them in schools designed to shape them in the Spartan mold. By contrast, in democratic Athens education was the responsibility of the parent and subject to parental choice and control. Schools were private, often owned by the teachers. The state's role was to specify minimal standards and to provide military training. Rather than destroy the family, as in Sparta, Athens preserved it as a means of developing and shaping personality and gave it responsibility for education. Athenians understood that this was vital in promoting a healthy sense of involvement in the community.[13] In terms of American values, the Athenian ideal is much to be preferrred over the Spartan.

Public schools do not have a true monopoly, of course; there are many private schools, both religious and nonreligious. They serve about a tenth of the children, and their enrollments have been rising as parents scrimp and save to send their children to them. But such parents are paying twice over for education, once through taxes to support the public schools they reject and once through tuition payments to the schools of their choice; the state service must be paid for whether used or not.

To reestablish parental choice in education in the United States today, perhaps the best way to start is to allow a tax deduction for tuition expenses. Tuition charges up to a certain amount should be free of federal, state, and local taxes, as proposed by Senator Moynihan.[14] This would permit a larger number of families to arrange for their children's education outside the state monopoly. The number can be increased in a second step by giving compensatory vouchers for partial or full tuition to low-income families. Subsequently, a full-fledged voucher system can be established, replacing the tax deduction. Public schools need not be shut down under this proposed system, but they would have to compete for their students, and therefore many would no doubt go under.

Unquestionably there is a need for broad consonance of basic societal goals and values, and a knowledge of shared history, but these do not require a government education monopoly; they can be realized even in a pluralistic educational system if government sets requirements for mastery of certain material in the curriculum and prescribes and administers standard tests to measure the performance of different schools. It would report individual scores to students and parents, and it would disseminate school averages broadly so that parents could take them into consideration when choosing schools for their children. Parents would have available, in effect, an analysis of education services, a hybrid of *Lovejoy's College Guide* and *Consumer Reports*. In this way the proper role of government is retained and even strengthened, for as an arranger or provider rather than a producer, government need not conspire or collude with its education arm and announce defensively that the educational function is being performed well and any problems rest elsewhere.

Coons and Sugarman have devoted considerable attention to designing a voucher system that avoids many of the potential problems that one can envision.[15] As to the charge that private schools are elite institutions and merely a subterfuge for racism and class segregation, the evidence does not support such an extreme view. In California, the nation's most populous state, private schools have a larger percentage of black and Hispanic children than do the public schools; in the Northeast, surprisingly, children in private schools and in public schools have similar distributions of family income.[16] While the proper concern that this system will encourage racial segregation cannot be dismissed out of hand, it can be argued persuasively that as a nation we are over the barrier for the most part, that both black and white parents see the main need now is to be better educated, and that over all the advantages outweigh the disadvantages. One must constantly remember that we are not designing paradise but merely trying to improve a bad situation. No doubt the system proposed here will, if implemented, exhibit serious defects in time and will itself require reform and replacement by a future system that better satisfies those future needs. No system man can devise will be good for all eternity.

Opposition to any change is to be expected of course, particularly to the idea of a voucher system, as Bridge has noted.[17] But education vouchers can be introduced gradually on a more limited basis, to parents of handicapped children, for example, and for on-the-job training in private firms. The latter is a superior alternative to conventional vocational education, for a private firm has an incentive to prepare a trainee for a real job and not for an obsolete craft. In Minneapolis, for example, a large computer firm competes with local schools to provide manpower training.

Communities could go further and gradually load-shed all vocational education, which at present inadequately performs the task that more properly belongs to employers. Any way one looks at it, such training is a private good that benefits the employer and the employee.

Indeed, in the field of adult or continuing education, one should recognize the growing role of the private sector: Business and industry spend more than $30 billion a year on educating and training their employees, a figure almost as large as the annual expenditures of the nation's public colleges and universities. Increasingly, firms offer accredited courses and even grant degrees. The largest private employer in the United States, AT&T, spends $1.1 billion on education, and on any given day 3 percent of its employees are in class.[18] It would not appear to be a major step for some firms to move fully into adult education, by opening enrollments to the public at large.

Private education programs have been criticized. In New York City, the numerous proprietary schools that offer training to would-be barbers, beauticians, computer programmers, cashiers, secretaries, truck drivers, and other job seekers are sometimes accused of flagrant abuses; they are charged with enrolling students who are incapable of doing the work and failing to find jobs for them. Nevertheless, in its open-admissions program the city's own university was also guilty of accepting students unable to do the work, as demonstrated by the high failure rate; municipal colleges are allowed to get away with blatantly misleading advertising that is prohibited for proprietary schools, and they made illegal campaign contributions of public funds to friendly legislators.[19] Moreover, one wonders whether the placement results of proprietary schools are any worse than those of public vocational schools.

One has to suspect the motives of those who would impose rigid and nearly fatal restrictions on proprietary schools, ostensibly to protect individuals from wasting their tuition money, while ignoring similar shortcomings in the public schools that result in a monumental waste of public money. Again, the focus of concern should not be whether private education has faults—of course it does—but how it compares with public education today.

This raises the related issue of the extent of compulsory education. Too many older teenagers are forced, against their wills, to enroll in schools—I say "enroll" advisedly, for many of them rarely attend, and truant officers are ineffective in getting them to do so. When they do attend, they are the principal causes of violence and disruption in schools, so that their presence results in less total education taking place than if they were absent. Why force someone to consume a good he does not want and which costs a lot to produce? Permitting students to end their formal schooling at an earlier age is likely to lead to improved education for those who choose to continue while opening up to the "dropouts"—a less pejorative term will be needed—opportunities for on the job training at public (via vouchers) or private (via wages) expense. The latter choice will require a more realistic minimum wage to be applied to such apprentices who are not yet fully productive workers. Remedial education opportunities should be available for them when and if, as adults, they desire to resume classroom learning.

Higher education lends itself readily to the ideas espoused here. That it is valued as a private good is clear from the extent to which personal savings and loans are utilized to pay for the cost of college. It is well known that, on the average, those who go to college will earn more over their lifetimes than those who don't (and most assume, perhaps in error, that this is a cause-effect relationship), and so the free market is widely used to deliver this obviously much-prized service.

In recognition of this self-evident fact, tuition charges in government universities should be increased to reflect more fully the true cost of this valuable service, and the cost of teaching should be distinguished from the cost of research. To the extent that political reality demands a subsidy for higher education, public funds should be used to expand low-interest, deferred-loan programs, which retain the essential features of the market for this service.

If a higher level of public expenditures for higher education is desired, then a voucher system should be employed. There is ample precedent and experience for this approach. When the number of vouchers issued is limited, they are called scholarships. The State of New York already has such a voucher program: It awards Regents Scholarships on the basis of competitive examinations to state residents, to be used in any institution of higher education in the state. As mentioned previously, the GI Bill offers further evidence that vouchers work well for higher education. It was a broad-based voucher system that was not very restricted, and it can serve as a model for government financing of higher education.

Some might object to this approach in the mistaken belief that low-income families would suffer. This is not the case at all. The poor subsidize the wealthy when it comes to higher education. Studies in Wisconsin and California show that the average income of families *with* children in the respective government universities is substantially greater than that of families without. The effect of these public universities is to "promote greater rather than less inequality among people of various social and economic backgrounds by making available substantial subsidies that lower income families are either not eligible for or cannot make use of. . . ."[20]

All these programs would accomplish the purpose of introducing competition to the sheltered public university systems. As long as financial factors play the dominant role in dictating college choice, the state universities need not worry about filling their classrooms and keeping their faculties occupied. The competition that would be engendered by these proposals would eliminate institutional torpor and produce long-term benefits to students and society.

Nevertheless, the political barriers to these reforms are large. Accordingly, Thompson and Fisk advocate a more modest approach that they believe is more acceptable politically and yet moves in the direction of increasing competition.[21] Applied to New York, their scheme would involve a base-level budget for the city university and a per-student grant in a fixed amount to any college in the city, public or private. In fact, the beginnings of such a system are already in place; the state government gives a fixed amount of money to any private university in the state for each degree awarded.

One is also starting to see a restoration of user charges for this private good below the college level. Tuition-charging summer school programs sprang up throughout California after Proposition 13 caused a shutdown of what was called the world's largest baby-sitting service—the summer program in public schools that was free for everyone.

It was finally recognized that summer programs cost money, relatively few children need academic help during the summer, and the vast majority of families can afford to pay a fee for recreation and enrichment programs to occupy their children during this period.[22]

Voucher Systems

As was illustrated above in connection with education, voucher systems can foster competition in the supply of those private and toll goods that are to be provided in whole or in part at collective expense. The optimal conditions under which a voucher system will work well for a particular service were summarized by Gary Bridge as follows:[23]

1. There are widespread differences in people's preferences for the service, and these differences are recognized and accepted by the public as legitimate.

2. Individuals have incentives to shop aggressively for the service.

3. Individuals are well informed about market conditions, including the cost and quality of the service and where it may be obtained.

4. There are many competing suppliers of the service or else start-up costs are low and additional suppliers can readily enter the market if the demand is there.

5. The quality of the service is easily measurable.

6. The service is relatively inexpensive and purchased frequently, so that the user learns by experience.

Bridge evaluated various voucher systems currently in effect or tried in the United States. He concluded that education vouchers for elementary and secondary education have little chance of success because of organized resistance by those in the "school business." By contrast, a voucher system for higher education, as suggested above, should be able to replicate the success of the GI Bill because (1) there are many colleges in competition for students; (2) the different colleges have markedly different reputations and specialties, and students can discriminate intelligently between them; (3) students are willing to attend colleges away from home, and this increases the effective number of colleges competing for any one student;(4) institutional income depends to a great extent on tuition payments, so schools have an incentive to attract and service students; (5) the vouchers do not cover the full cost of higher education, so students have an incentive to shop aggressively for the best school at the best price.

The food stamp program comes closest to being a true voucher system, as are culture vouchers in New York City where there are hundreds of competing cultural institutions. (Individuals receive subsidized tickets and have a choice of several different kinds of performances.) However, Medicare and Medicaid fall short of satisfying the above-stated ideal conditions for the use of vouchers: Consumers have no incentive to shop, competition by service providers is conspicuously absent due to regulation by state agencies and medical societies, and the quality of service is difficult to gauge. Vouchers that would replace Medicaid and enable poor people to purchase health insurance offer the prospect of ending the inflationary pressure on health-care costs and bringing them under control.

Other areas where vouchers might be used, Bridge suggests, are in transportation, child care, and legal services. The elderly poor in transit-poor suburbs could be issued vouchers that would be accepted as payment by transportation suppliers such as bus and taxi companies and even private cars. Parents with child-care vouchers could place their children in day-care centers that provided the best combination of price and service. Indigent defendants could use vouchers to obtain legal assistance instead of having to rely on either the government's public defender or grant-subsidized legal-aid units.

Vouchers—that is, subsidies to consumers—are better than grants—that is, subsidies to producers—in that they enhance citizen choice. Some would argue, therefore, that poor people should be given the ultimate voucher, cash, to further strengthen individual choice and responsibility. However, there is a pitfall along this path. People have limited capacity to consume food and shelter, but they have an unlimited capacity to consume money. Moreover, as noted on page 125, if the money is not spent in ways acceptable to the providers of the money—taxpayers or bureaucrats—the pressure to appoint guardians and control the spending will be irresistible, and the result will be larger and costlier government.

Contracting or Purchase of Service

As illustrated in chapter 4, many services can be procured by contract from the private sector, a process that offers an excellent opportunity to introduce and institutionalize competition by employing procedures such as competitive bidding.

Competition can be sharpened even further when the public and private sectors both deliver the same service in the same jurisdiction; that is, when mixed and multiple arrangements are utilized. In such cases the results are likely to be particularly beneficial to the public. For example, the cities of Montreal, Minneapolis, Phoenix, New Orleans, Kansas City, Newark, and Oklahoma City have such mixed systems for residential refuse collection. They employ contracts with private firms to service several districts of the city and a municipal department to service the remainder. In effect, the city agency bids against the private firms. The resulting competition has been successful in producing operating efficiencies and costs that are remarkably low by national standards. In Minneapolis city officials assiduously cultivated a competitive climate and, by pointing to the superior practices of the private crews, were able to get the city crews to adopt similar practices and ultimately to match their performance.[24]

The result, noted in chapter 6, that private firms under contract collect refuse more efficiently than government agencies, is probably due more to the difference between competitive and monopoly provision of the service than to the difference between private and public delivery. Public service has the characteristic of a permanent monopoly, while contract service can be thought of as a system of periodic competition, and the free market offers permanent competition. In refuse collection there is strong reason to prefer contract collection instead of municipal collection or free market private collection; the former is significantly more efficient than the latter two, which are equally inefficient.[25] The reason why the market arrangement, which features continuous competition, is—contrary to one's initial expectation—inferior to the contract system, which is characterized by periodic competition or temporary monopoly, is that (1) it is inefficient to have several different trucks from several different firms collecting from residences on the same street, and (2) it is more costly for a private firm to bill each individual residential customer than to bill a single government agency. The contract collector is awarded, in effect, a temporary monopoly to service every house in the area, but the contract is of limited duration, typically two or three years, and is awarded competitively. Unlike a city agency, the contractor who wins the award has no assurance that he will continue to do the work forever; he cannot become complacent and must aim for continued or improved efficiency and effective service if he is to win out in the next competition.

Contracting for a service that requires long-lived capital assets presents a problem, although not an insuperable one. How will someone who has been awarded a contract for three years amortize a facility he's had to build that has a twenty-year life? The most direct approach would be to set the term of the contract equal to the life of the assets. This approach is tantamount to granting a long-term monopoly, however, and has little to commend it. Another approach is to recognize that the asset can be depreciated over time, has a value at any point in time, and can be sold to the new service producer if the original one is unsuccessful in bidding for a successor contract. Yet another approach is to have the government own the long-lived asset and lease it to the successful bidder at a price stated in the request for bids. This could be done for buses, garages, restaurants and service stations on turnpikes, and facilities for concessions in parks and stadiums.

In deciding whether to contract for service, a government unit should compare the costs of government and contract service. This is not as easy to do as it might appear. Typically, the cost of government service is taken to be the cost stated in the budget. Government budgets are not designed to be used for cost accounting purposes, however, and are inadequate for such use because they usually fail to include significant expenses such as fringe benefits and capital costs. A study of this issue in sixty-eight cities found that the true cost of a government service was 30 percent higher than indicated in the budget.[26]

Given the magnitude of this misperception, one can expect that incorrect conclusions will often result from analyses that rely on budgets to compare the cost of government and contract service provision. The cards are likely to be stacked in favor of the government producer when an attempt is made, in effect, to have both the government and the private producer bid to do the job.

The true cost of service emerged as a major point of contention in efforts to "contract out" more federal government functions. Prior to 1976, for the purpose of comparing government to contract costs the total cost of retirement benefits for federal employees was considered to be 7 percent of gross pay. This unbelievably low figure was recalculated in 1976, and was found to be 24.7 percent of gross pay. Federal employees fought vigorously against this realistic guideline and actually succeeded a year later in getting this figure (but not their benefits, of course!) reduced to 14.1 percent of gross wages; later it was raised to 20.4 percent and in the most recent guidelines it was set at 26 percent.[27]

In order to limit the potential for contracting out federal functions, a representative of the civil servants ingeniously noted that the Social Security System is seriously underfunded and therefore, since additional social security costs will ultimately be incurred by the government when workers retire from the private sector, this amount should be added to the price of the contract itself for the purpose of making comparisons between government and contract work. He also asked that the cost of unemployment compensation for discharged federal workers be added to the contract price, but failed to note that, correspondingly, unemployment compensation would end for any workers hired by the private sector to perform the contract work; presumably these costs and savings balance out each other. However, he made the excellent recommendation that a competitive cost analysis be performed for every proposed contract and made public.[28]

Civil servants also tried to insert into the guidelines addi-. tional restrictions, whose net effect was to impose cumbersome bureaucratic barriers and thereby to discourage managers in government agencies from undertaking any effort to contract for service. For example, they called for the creation of a central agency to oversee all proposed contracts and the preparation of social impact statements for each proposal.[29]

The federal guidelines set a savings threshold; that is, contracting should be done only if the expected savings exceeded 10 percent of the personnel-related cost of performing the work in-house. At the same time, agencies that wished to assume functions performed by a contractor would have to demonstrate that they could save at least 10 percent on personnel costs and 25 percent on the cost of facilities and materials that the government would have to begin providing. Agencies were further required to take into consideration the federal taxes paid by a contractor; these constituted a rebate, in effect, and led to a lower net cost to the government than the stated bid price.

As to the potential for contracting out federal services, Congressman Kemp reported that 18,618 federal government activities provided a product or service that was available from the private sector; this corresponded to $7 billion annually of in-house work that could be contracted to the private sector, at a projected saving of $850 million a year.[30] The Reagan administration estimates that as many as 226,000 jobs out of the federal civilian work force of about 2 million could be turned over to the private sector.[31]

Robert Poole presents an intriguing scenario of the fictitious city in California that over twenty years, gradually contracted out all its services.[32] It started with a contract for private fire protection after the city experienced a serious fire while its firemen were on strike. Following a grand jury indictment of the police chief, in Poole's vivid tale, the city entered into a contract with the county sheriff for police services. In short order, thereafter, street, park, and vehicle maintenance were contracted to private firms, followed by building inspection, sewage treatment, and water supply. Then a private guard service replaced the county sheriff. Next, the city sold off its docks, beaches, and parking lots to private operators and its parks to local neighborhood associations. Finally, City Hall itself was sold, and the remaining three employees rented a small office to oversee and manage the contracts. (They had to charge for the time they spent with the incredulous researchers and outside officials who swarmed in to see how the city achieved such a low per capita cost and such a high growth rate with full employment.) This fictitious example is not so far-fetched: La Mirada, California, a city of 40,000 people, contracts out over 60 essential services, and has only 55 employees.[33]

Contract Specifications

To purchase services requires careful preparation of contract specifications. A contractor cannot respond intelligently to a poorly drawn request for bids, and if he does, subsequent misunderstandings are inevitable. The instance was cited in chapter 6 where a federal government facility that ostensibly sought to contract out its laundry operation did not know how many pieces had to be ironed and could not inform prospective bidders. On the other hand, some agencies go too far and prepare specifications that go beyond stating performance requirements and specify irrelevancies as to how the contractor should carry out the work. For example, some misguided specifications for refuse collection contracts call for particular kinds of vehicles to be used, the number of men to work on each truck, the wages to be paid, and the union to be recognized. Clearly, such specifications transgress the bounds of management prerogatives and obviate the entire purpose of contracting for service, which may indeed be the underlying intention of those who draw up such self-defeating contract terms.

This is one of the barriers to contracting for service—setting specifications whose hidden purpose or ultimate effect is to make contract service as costly as government service, thereby eliminating the incentive to change. Other obstacles include tradition, employee opposition, the difficulty of writing specifications for some services, the limited number of suppliers in some services, and possible legal restrictions with respect to matching funds. For example, a local government that receives a federal matching grant for a program may wish to use city overhead expenditures as part of its matching contribution. This may or may not be acceptable to federal auditors if the service is contracted to a private organization.

On the other side of the coin, it is generally easy to write specifications that favor a particular bidder, and hence there is room for corrupt practices.

So-called "hard" services, those involving tangible and visible physical results, are generally easier to write specifications for than the kind of "soft" services provided by social workers to clients. But even the former can be difficult to do. For example, whereas street paving is a good candidate for competitive contracting, repair of potholes is not as good. The reason is that information on the location and frequency of pothole occurrence, and on the expected life of repaved streets, is virtually nonexistent in most cities. How, then, can one write specifications for such work? A contractor cannot respond sensibly to a specification that calls for "the repair of all potholes that may occur on a given street" nor to a broader specification "to maintain a given street free of potholes," for in the latter case he cannot intelligently weigh the tradeoffs of repaving the street or fixing the potholes. Finally, because it is technically difficult to identify individual potholes, letting a contract on a "per pothole" basis is inviting trouble. Pothole repair by municipal crews, with good supervision, is probably best unless the entire street can be made the responsibility of a neighborhood group.

One reason why the number of potential suppliers is sometimes low is the dilatory behavior of some governments in paying their bills. Consider a city that, over the past century, constructed an elaborate, time-consuming, costly, bureaucratic system of checks and balances designed to assure that it received fair value in its purchases and was protected against corruption in contracting for supplies and equipment. However, the consequence is a long delay in securing bids, ordering goods, and paying bills. Requests are prepared and submitted to bidders on an approved list. Sealed bids are received and opened ceremoniously, contracts are awarded, purchase orders are prepared and issued, goods are received, several different agencies check to see that the right goods are delivered in good condition to the right place at the right time, payment is authorized after a proper invoice is received and then cross-checked, and finally a check for payment is grudgingly issued by the city treasury many months later.

The result of all this red tape is that many potential vendors refuse to do business with the city, while those who do deal with the city have to charge higher prices to make up for their additional costs and trouble. A strategy intended to *increase* competition and *reduce* the cost of goods has precisely the opposite effect of *reducing* competition and *increasing* costs.

Contract Award

The ideal is to have many competing suppliers; award enough contracts both to avoid excessive reliance on a single supplier and to permit a significant fraction of the bidders to succeed in their quest, thereby encouraging the losers to try again next time; award few enough contracts so that the administrative burden is manageable; have the contracts small enough so that disaster does not strike someone who had a contract and lost it; have the contracts large enough to allow economies of scale; and handle problems and pay bills promptly to keep suppliers interested in holding on to the business.

To assure serious bidding and effective contract performance, it is common to require bid bonds and performance bonds. The former is forfeited if the bidder declines the award, and the latter is forfeited if the contractor defaults during the contract period. The size of the performance bond should not be set at a punitively high level, which simply increases the cost of the contract unnecessarily; it should be sufficient merely to defray the cost of making other arrangements to have the work done.[34] A performance bond is best thought of as an insurance policy whose premium is ultimately paid by the contracting authority.

It is worth noting, in passing, that although competitive bidding is legally required in many jurisdictions, and such a procedure cannot readily be faulted, there is some empirical evidence that negotiated bids lead to prices that are no higher than competitive bids.[35]

As to the type of contract, there are several alternative ways to provide incentives for good performance and to handle uncertainties. Cost-plus-fixed-fee is at one end of the spectrum of contract types, and firm-fixed-price-with-incentives is at the other.[36] The former appears to lead to a minimal price but has no incentive to encourage efficiency and much disincentive.

Contract Monitoring

Contracting for service has its problems, of course. There are costs involved in preparing specifications, bid requests, and contracts, and there are costs involved in monitoring the performance of the contractor. (In one well-studied service, refuse collection, monitoring costs ranged from 1 percent to 5 percent of the contract price.) It should be remembered that there are also monitoring costs for government services, including the cost of city and state controllers, for example.

There is also the possibility that because of poor contract administration, the competitive factor will be weakened and the contract service permitted to degenerate into a private monopoly, which would be no improvement over a public one. Owners of firms have been known to get together with their employees and to demand an increase in the contract price to pay for "unanticipated" wage increases, under the threat of a strike. A private-sector union sometimes serves as the vehicle for assuring noncompetitive practices and conspiratorial, collusive bidding. The best defense against such occurrences is to have part of the work done by a government agency and part by contractors—the more the better, up to a point. The performance of the public agency serves as a yardstick to measure the performance of the private agency, and vice versa. If the private sector shows signs that its competitive spirit is waning, government can expand the size and scope of the public unit's work and correspondingly reduce the size of the contract. In fact, the threat of greatly reducing the role of either the public or private producer is a most effective check on both, as is the ability to use one to intervene on an emergency basis to do the work of the other if the latter is unable or unwilling to perform, due to strikes or equipment malfunction, for example. Montreal has developed this to a fine art and has a well-defined rate schedule to cover the cost of municipal intervention if a contractor fails to collect refuse or clear snow on schedule in his assigned area. The plausible threat of municipal intervention, and the occasional need to do so—for a day or two every couple of years—has been sufficient to guarantee excellent performance by the city's fifty-odd contractors, while the fact that the municipal agency does only 10 percent of the work means that the city can readily have a contractor substitute for the city agency if necessary.

CONCLUSION

It is evident that the four strategies presented in this chapter— load shedding, arrangements that require minimal government involvement, user charges, and competition—reinforce one another and can be blended together. A decline in the quantity or quality of service leads some citizens to seek out or devise alternatives to supply or supplant the service. This invites load shedding. User charges provide information that facilitates evaluation and accelerates the process. Contracting and vouchers encourage competition and promote efficiency, and can be employed in concert with load shedding.

Implementation of these strategies is already happening. That is, one can discern patterns in current events that are in conformance with these strategies. Thus, while no one would dream of abolishing a police department, voluntary citizen patrols are becoming ever more commonplace in large cities that have crime problems. Government is not abandoning its concern for solid-waste management; on the contrary, its involvement is increasing, but increasingly it is the private sector that local governments turn to for treating hazardous wastes, for disposing of wastes at sophisticated, environmentally sound landfills, for extracting energy and recyclables from waste in technologically advanced resource recovery facilities, and for collecting the waste efficiently and effectively in the first place.

The major opposition to these strategies comes from determined groups of public employees, for the most part, but their strength and success in opposing these strategies depends on public support or at least indifference. Public support of teachers has not yet waned sufficiently to permit education vouchers to get very far, but support of many other conventional local agencies is now so weak that political leaders are often able to overcome employee resistance and impose these policies; for example, contracting out of refuse collection services was found to occur with surprising ease in a series of case studies.[37]

Inflation can become an ally in the effort to reduce government growth if spending caps and balanced budgets are imposed, tax cuts are passed, and tax brackets are indexed to inflation so that government revenues do not grow disproportionately. In this setting, fixed-dollar limits on taxes and spending, or limits that do not keep pace with inflation, would have the effect of reducing the relative size and role of government.

In summary, public services can be provided through a broad array of mechanisms, most of which involve government in a more limited role than conventional thinking allows. Wider use of these alternative mechanisms requires a reorientation and revision in attitudes about the relative responsibilities of government, the individual, voluntary associations, and the marketplace. Load shedding, together with greater reliance on nongovernmental arrangements and the introduction of competition through voucher systems and by contracting, are policies that have enormous potential for restricting and reversing the growth of government, improving the delivery of public services, and enhancing the lot of citizens.

NOTES

1. "Subsidized Paint," *New York Times,* 21 April 1979, p. 26.
2. "Regan Sees Housing-Default Peril," *New York Times,* 3 May 1979, p. A1.
3. "An Expensive Housing Experiment," *Public Interest,* no. 56 (Summer 1979).
4. Michael Knight, "Boston Housing Authority Placed in Receivership," *New York Times,* 26 July 1979, p. A12.
5. Peter F. Drucker, "Can the Businessman Meet Our Social Needs?" *Saturday Review,* April 1973.
6. Robert W. Poole, Jr., "Rethinking Building Codes," *Fiscal Watchdog,* no. 29 (March 1979). Local Government Center, Santa Barbara, Calif.
7. Lyle C. Fitch, "Increasing the Role of the Private Sector in Providing Public Services," in *Improving the Quality of Urban Management,* ed. Willis D. Hawley and David Rogers (Beverly Hills, Calif.: Sage, 1974).
8. See the publications of Public Service Options, Minneapolis, Minn., for further discussion of these ideas.
9. Nan Robertson, "France Divides State TV Network into Rival Units," *New York Times,* 4 July 1974.
10. E.S. Savas, "Municipal Monopolies Versus Competition

in Delivering Urban Services," in Hawley and Rogers, *Improving the Quality of Urban Management.*

11. William D. Burt, *Local Problems, Libertarian Solutions* (Washington, D.C.: Libertarian Party, 1978).

12. Murray N. Rothbard, *For a New Liberty* (New York: Macmillan, 1978), p. 126.

13. Richard E. Wagner, "American Education and the Economics of Caring," in *Parents, Teachers, and Children: Prospects for Choice in American Education* (San Francisco: Institute for Contemporary Studies, 1977).

14. Daniel Patrick Moynihan, "Government and the Ruin of Private Education," *Harper's Magazine,* April 1978, pp. 28-38.

15. John E. Coons and Stephen D. Sugarman, *Family Choice in Education: A Model State System for Vouchers* (Berkeley: University of California, Institute of Governmental Studies, 1971).

16. Thomas Vitullo-Martin, "New York City's Interest in Reform of Tax Treatment of School Expenses," *City Almanac* 13, no. 4 (December 1978).

17. Gary Bridge, "Citizen Choice in Public Services: Voucher Systems," in *Alternatives for Delivering Public Services: Toward Improved Performance,* ed. E.S. Savas (Boulder, Colo.: Westview Press, 1977).

18. Gene I. Maeroff, "Business Is Cutting into the Market," *New York Times,* 30 August 1981, sec. 12, p. 1.

19. Edward B. Fiske, "Schools for Profit," *New York Times,* 26 July 1979, p. B1; "State Seeks Tighter Control of Vocational Education," *New York Times,* 27 July 1979, p. B1; "Playing Politics with Public Money," *New York Times,* editorial, 7 November 1980.

20. Rothbard, *For a New Liberty,* p. 138.

21. Fred Thompson and Gary Fiske, "One More Solution to the Problem of Higher Education," *Policy Analysis* 4, no. 4 (Fall 1978): 577-80.

22. Robert W. Poole, Jr., "Toward Free Public Education," *Fiscal Watchdog,* no. 33 (July 1979). National Taxpayers Union, Santa Barbara, Calif.

23. Bridge, "Citizen Choice in Public Services."

24. E.S. Savas, "An Empirical Study of Competition in Municipal Service Delivery," *Public Administration Review* 37, no. 6 (November/December 1977): 717-24.

25. E.S. Savas, "Policy Analysis for Local Government: Public vs. Private Refuse Collection," *Policy Analysis* 3, no. 1 (Winter 1977): 49-74.
26. E.S. Savas, "How Much Do Government Services Really Cost? *Urban Affairs Quarterly* 15, no. 1 (September 1979): 23-42.
27. U.S. Office of Management and Budget, Circular No. A-76, Washington, D.C., 29 March 1979.
28. James M. Pierce, Statement, *Hearings on Contracting Out of Jobs and Services, Subcommittee on Employee Ethics and Utilization, Committee on Post Office and Civil Service, House of Representatives,* Serial No. 95-7 (Washington, D.C.: U.S. Government Printing Office, 1977), pp. 41-43.
29. Ibid.
30. Congressman Jack Kemp, ibid., pp. 47-48; the capital investment cost of these activities amount to $2 billion, according to the statement of the administrator of Federal Procurement Policy, *Hearings before Senate Government Operations Committee, Subcommittee on Federal Spending Practices, Efficiency, and Open Government,* 24 August 1976.
31. David B. Smith, "OMB Presses for More Contracting Out," *National Journal,* 6 June 1981, p. 1032.
32. Robert W. Poole, Jr., "Looking Back: How City Hall Withered," in *Cutting Back City Hall* (New York: Universe Books, 1980).
33. "La Mirada: A City with a Different View," *Government Executive Magazine,* May 1981, pp. 47-48.
34. Bennett C. Jaffee, "Contracts for Residential Refuse Collection," in *The Organization and Efficiency of Solid Waste Collection,* ed. E.S. Savas (Lexington, Mass.: Lexington Books, 1977).
35. Franklin R. Edwards and Barbara J. Stevens, "The Provision of Municipal Sanitation Services by Private Firms: An Empirical Analysis of the Efficiency of Alternative Market Structures and Regulatory Arrangements," *Journal of Industrial Economics* 27, no. 2 (December 1978): 133-47.
36. James L. Mercer and Edwin H. Koester, *Public Management Systems* (New York: AMACOM, 1978), pp. 177-85.
37. Eileen B. Berenyi, "Privatization of Residential Refuse Collection Services: A Study of Institutional Change," *Urban Interest* 3, no. 1 (Spring 1981): 30-42.

INDEX